Medieval Women Mystics

Medieval Women Mystics

Gertrude the Great
Angela of Foligno
Birgitta of Sweden
Julian of Norwich

Elizabeth Ruth Obbard, editor

NEW CITY PRESS
Hyde Park, NY

For Sr. Norah Rohan, FMDM
In gratitude for many years of friendship

Published in the United States by New City Press
202 Cardinal Rd., Hyde Park, NY 12538
Www.newcitypress.com
© New City Press 2002/2007

Cover design by Leandro de Leon

Library of Congress Cataloging-in-Publication Data:

Medieval women mystics : Gertrude the great, Angela of Foligno, Birgitta of Sweden,
Julian of Norwich / [edited by] Elizabeth Ruth Obbard.
    p. cm.
Includes bibliographical references.
ISBN 978-1-56548-278-4
    1. Women mystics. 2. Mysticism--History--Middle Ages, 600-1500. 3. Spiritual
life--Christianity--History of doctrines--Middle Ages, 600-1500. I. Obbard, Elizabeth
Ruth, 1945-

BV5095.A1 M43 2001   2001051216
248.2'2'0922-dc21

1st printing: March 2002
2nd printing (rev. ed.): August 2007

Printed in the United States of America

Contents

Introduction

The period of the Crusades, beginning with the entry of Godefroye de Bouillon into Jerusalem in 1099, opened an era in Europe's history which affected all areas of life, not least the life of women. The growth of trade fueled by contact with the East, and the opening up of new trade routes, did much to increase interest in foreign travel, including pilgrimage. Concomitantly, the rapid growth of a new merchant class coupled with a general movement toward the cities eroded the sense of stability that had characterized feudal attachment to the land and a life attuned to the rhythm of the seasons.

Many men, drawn by the lure of riches and glory as well as spiritual gain, took the cross and departed for the Holy Land as crusaders, while the women they left behind were rapidly forming a new group to be reckoned with. No longer was interest in religious life only possible for the nobility and the aristocracy who could afford the large dowries expected for entering a convent. These new women—wives, mothers, sisters, daughters of merchants and skilled craftsmen (the rising middle class) had money, a modicum of education, practical skills, and they wanted to make a difference to society.

New religious movements took over from the older monastic model. The mendicant friars, inspired principally by Francis of Assisi and Dominic de Guzman, professed the *vita apostolica*, a form of religious life which combined mobility (after the mode of the apostles who traveled around with Christ) with prayer and service to the poor. In many places this now became more popular than the traditional Benedictine path, comprising a life dominated by the singing of the Divine Office and scholarly pursuits within one monastery where the monk would remain for life.

The interest in the Holy Land aroused by the crusaders meant that the direct imitation of Christ took on an importance heretofore unknown. It was reflected in the increased number of hermits and anchorites who eschewed organized conventual life in favor of their own calling to poverty and identification with the human Christ, who chose a life of poverty and labor in the midst of his contemporaries.

Between 1100 and 1400 the number of women saints rose substantially as women began to explore new roles within church and society. As they were still unable to hold official leadership positions in the hierarchical structure they took on the prophetic role, finding the courage to be generative in a variety of ways other than the physical childbearing expected of them.

Prominent among the new forms of religious life was that of the beguines, the first specifically women's movement which arose in the wake of the religious revival of the thirteenth century. Beguines were women not attached to any specific Order (though many linked themselves to the friars in various ways). They were not nuns, and were not generally from that strata of society which formed the backbone of the great women's communities following the Rule of Saint Benedict.

Beguines, who were prominent in Northern Europe, were women who chose dedicated lives in a variety of ways. Some lived at home, some with others. Some dedicated themselves to prayer, some combined prayer with works of charity and mercy. A woman who became a beguine put on a form of dress that singled her out as a person dedicated to God, but she did not make life vows. Instead she promised chastity while she remained in the beguinage. It was a feminine response to the popularity of the *vita apostolica* among men, and it aroused a certain amount of suspicion.

As the life of a beguine was flexible it could take various forms, and relied for its efficacy on personal devotion rather than traditional rules and structures. Mechtild of Magdeburg, the only beguine mentioned in this collection went to Magdeburg to live as a beguine at the age of twelve, and remained there until she retired to the monastery of Helfta in old age. "Your childhood was a companion of the Holy Spirit; your youth was a bride of humanity; in your old age you are the humble housewife of the Godhead" the Lord said to her as she wondered how her life-story hung together. Angela of Foligno was the Southern European equivalent of a beguine, joining the Franciscan Third Order and choosing a lifestyle that she felt was suited to her particular calling. But whether beguines or not, all the women in this present study would have been influenced by the new approach; and the sight of women taking charge of their own lives in a variety of ways opened up horizons of activity and thought that were unfamiliar to women of earlier times.

Another influence that affected women in the period of the Crusades was the notion of romantic love fostered by the code of chivalry, where the Christian knight promised to protect and show respect for the vulnerable and weak of society, especially women and children. Popular tales of romance now portrayed women as love objects, in a relationship that was longed for but unconsummated for the most part (since marriage remained the domain of family and inheritance rather than romantic attachment). This fired women of God, especially the beguines, with a loving ardor, a romantic attachment to God, that spilled over into the lives of women following other religious paths.

The outpourings of Saint Gertrude, which originate in her relating to God precisely *as woman*, the sensuous passion of Angela of Foligno, the overwhelming desire of Birgitta to be acknowledged as "bride of the Lord," the independence and originality of Julian of Norwich, show how each one was influenced in her own way by the new perception of women and their place in society. Alongside this, many women were finding themselves marginalized by the establishment; Angela and Birgitta were already discovering that they needed to have their insights validated by men if they were to be heard. Angela's reliance on Brother Arnaldo and Birgitta's on Peter of Alvastra are cases in point.

After a brief flowering of literary and spiritual fervor the beguines were mostly absorbed into existing Orders and placed under male supervision, or their communities were dispersed. One beguine, Marguerite Porete, writer of *The Mirror of Simple Souls* was burned along with her book. Another, Hadewych, has only recently been rediscovered, although at this point in time it is impossible to reconstruct her life in any detail.

What is important in all the women mystics of this period is their growing sense of being women of God, able to relate to God in terms of deep intimacy. "Revelations" or mystical experiences were ways in which they could validate their teaching role. Formal education for women was still minimal except in extraordinary cases such as that of Gertrude, where the educational tradition in her abbey was far above average (and was not destined to outlast her for many years). Most women mystics had to rely on scribes or confessors who would record their words and translate them into Latin.

Because in their mystical experiences women involved the whole of their senses, including their sexuality, their writings have often been neglected in favor of more intellectually oriented theology. Only now are we coming to see that women have an irreplaceable role in bringing back a balance to spirituality. In them love, rather than theoretical truth, holds the primacy; or one could say that for them love was the arbiter of truth. Truth was found in loving response not in books of theology. For this reason women tended to stress the humanity of Christ, Christ's Eucharistic presence as their means of union with the flesh of the Beloved, and the place of Mary, woman of sorrows, virgin and mother, as their model.

Bernard of Clairvaux writes movingly on the Song of Songs, for example, but with him the bride is the image of the soul. For Bernard the soul is feminine to God whether one is man or woman. Women mystics, on the other hand, see their bridal mysticism as deeply entwined in their relating to God as whole persons, not as disembodied "souls." Christ Jesus the Lord is the one to whom they are betrothed, and their brideship consists in a love relationship of ardent response and surrender, each one in her own unique way. For Gertrude it is by way of Christ's wounded heart, for Angela by way of the cross and passion. For Birgitta and Julian their love for the Savior is translated into words of power, lived out in particular lifestyles that reflect their understanding of what it means to be called and chosen.

Each woman mystic, whether I have included them in this book or not (and obviously I have had to select from many possible choices) stresses the human reality of Christ and the concrete reality of other persons. We all exist in a context of community and family, and in this every woman is aware of her interrelatedness with others. She is not a theologian of the abstract but of the concrete here and now: Gertrude among her sisters at Helfta, Angela among her disciples and among the poor, Birgitta with her family bonds and mission to reform and legislate in practical ways, Julian as one of the "ordinary Christians" for whom she wrote and whom she saw as called to holiness through means of the daily love and service of God and neighbor.

Anne Belford Ulanov has noted that one of the aspects women bring to religion is their experience of pain. Women have the closest possible association with pain, not only through child-bearing but also because historically they have been marginalized and their experience not taken seriously.[1] Instead of holding on to grievances, the women mystics knew how to transmute their suffering into an identification with the outcast and Crucified Jesus. Often they protested that they were "only women," and yet one feels that was more to placate possible critics than a reflection of their true self-image. Christ had called them and validated them. They knew "from the inside" that they were loved. What comes through in their writings is a wholeness of being. They are affirmed as women who follow Christ with love and compassion, since they too have known suffering.

Women tend to grow and develop spiritually on a spiral or circular rather than a linear model.[2] This means that they keep returning to their inner processes, going deeper and deeper at one or a few points, rather than progressing along a linear path such as the traditional purgatorial, illuminative and unitive ways. Gertrude and Julian especially mirror this circular pattern—Gertrude in her reliving the mystery of the Incarnation ever more deeply among her sisters as her life unfolds within the stable monastic liturgical cycle; Julian in that she writes on the strength of one "mystical experience" at the point of presumed death, and spends the rest of her life drawing out its meaning. In this she re-examines her basic experience over and over again, teasing out from it, not new insights, but insights that are hidden in the one manifestation of the love of God as seen in the living and crucified Savior.

What women excel in when they are true to their own nature, as Julian so aptly teaches through her own life, is that womanly quality of waiting. A woman psychoanalyst who had worked with Jung wrote:

> The feminine in every woman is always waiting. She may not know it if she has a more masculine side which is busy with active achievement but I believe that every woman, if she looks deep enough, will find that the essential core of her is waiting. . . .
>
> Her lover emerges from the mists of time and in his wake also does the place where she will dwell. Whether it is near her birthplace or on a distant shore will be determined for her by the love to which she has been elected. It could not be foretold or planned. So she needs to wait, and the more conscious women know for what they wait.[3]

Maybe there are more women mystics than men because women are naturally more disposed to wait, to give time, to allow life and relationships to unfold in their own way and according to their own pattern.

The women in this book knew that they were gifted by God in a special manner. But they were also very aware that this gift was a grace that could not be earned. No love relationship can be forced, least of all a love relationship with God. They were aware that they had been called to intimacy with the Holy One. Their part was to surrender, to wait on God, to try to respond as fully as possible to grace offered.

Mystical graces cannot be forced. They are not something that can be acquired through deep breathing exercises or simply "willing" that they happen. One is "elected into love" not just for oneself but for others. That is why each woman in this book felt compelled to cry out that what she had experienced, what she "knew" in her very heart and flesh, was not just for herself but was "gift" also for others who heard her speak or who would read her works. These women were like the wise virgins who kept the sacred oil of love always alight in their lamps, ready for the bridegroom's coming, even though they could not predict the time or the hour of his visitation. Their business was to remain alert; and from that experience of waiting, surrendering, receiving, they were able to gather up the whole of their fragmented lives into an integrated response that affected their entire person.

While there are specific qualities that women excel in and which make them particularly open to certain types of mystical experience, it would be a mistake to think that every religious woman is gifted in this way, or that those so gifted are like one another. Rather, in her relationship with God and others each person is called to become more herself and more individual. Reading the women mystics in this book is to encounter very different lifestyles, very different ways of responding to grace, because each one's personal history is unique and unrepeatable.

So in reading their words we should not want to duplicate the experiences recorded therein but see them as challenges and pointers toward our own personal relationship with God and with those among whom we live. Mysticism is for all, for it is basically about allowing Christ to live in us and make his home within us. Holiness is not about paranormal states or visions, it is about Christ-bearing translated into daily life. If the women in this book had failed in their primary calling to holiness they would have nothing to say to us today. As it is they challenge our mediocrity by the witness of their whole lives. They were compelled to cry out, for our sake, that God exists, that God loves us, and that God demands from us a response that brooks no compromise.

Notes

1. A. Belford Ulanov, *Receiving Woman: Studies in the Psychology and Theology of the Feminine* (Philadelphia: Westminster, 1981), 151.

2. L. Byrne, *Women Before God* (London: SPCK, 1988), 69.

3. I. Claremont de Castillejo, *Knowing Woman: A Feminine Psychology* (London: Hodder & Stoughton, 1973), 172.

Gertrude the Great

1256–1302

Introduction

The Benedictine Abbey of Helfta was the home of three noteworthy medieval women: Mechtild of Magdeburg, Mechtild of Helfta, and Gertrude "the great." Mechtild of Magdeburg was an erstwhile beguine, writer of *The Flowing Light of the Godhead*, who sought refuge among Helfta's sisters when she became old and blind; Mechtild of Helfta was sister to the abbess, a respected member of the community, and herself a visionary with a beautiful voice; for many years she was first chantress and leader of the monastic choir. Gertrude was the youngest and most famous of the trio who all lived in the same vibrant community of women. Gertrude's writings have been widely disseminated and, although she was never formally canonized, her feast day is observed by the universal church on November 17.

The abbey of Helfta was founded initially in Rodersdorf, Saxony, but moved to Helfta (also in Saxony) in 1258, where the ancestral seat of the Hackeborn family was established. Mechtild and her older sister, the abbess Gertrude (not to be confused with our Gertrude) belonged to this aristocratic clan, and Helfta was soon known as a community where secular and spiritual learning went hand in hand in the very best

Benedictine tradition. The piety was ardent, and the sisters seem to have been much influenced by the newly founded Cistercian Order, whose greatest advocate, Bernard of Clairvaux, introduced a strong romantic element into personal prayer and the celebration of the liturgy, together with a renewed emphasis on the importance of community life. Study was held in honor among these women. Their school was renowned for its breadth of classical and religious learning, and Mechtild's glorious voice, which led the singing of the Offices of the church, was so admired that she was given the appellation "God's nightingale."

At the age of twelve Mechtild had gone to visit her sister, already a nun at the abbey of Rodersdorf, and begged to stay on among the community for her education. As a young nun of twenty, two years after the move to Helfta under her sister, Mechtild was placed in charge of the pupils in the abbey school. One day a five-year-old was brought to the nuns as a child oblate and given into Mechtild's care. The girl was Gertrude, whose parentage remains unknown to us. As the abbey harbored a number of aristocratic women, proud of their family lineage, it is probable that Gertrude was either an orphan or the love child of some lord, placed among the nuns for safety and for a suitable upbringing, in the hope that not too many questions would be asked about her background. As far as we know Gertrude never knew any of her own relatives, and so the community was her home and family from infancy onward. The Lord himself said of Gertrude in later life that it was solely on his account that she was so loved, as she had no family name, no prestigious title, with which to claim a privileged position among the Benedictine ladies from Saxony's best families.

Mechtild, although fifteen years older than Gertrude, was drawn to her young pupil, and between the two a deep friendship was to spring up. Gertrude later recorded Mechtild's spiritual experiences by writing of them in *The Book of Special Grace*, and Mechtild praised Gertrude in her turn. It was a true friendship of intimate love, support, care and respect, although each was not blind to the other's faults, as can be seen in the rather humorous exchange where Mechtild asks the Lord why he allowed Gertrude to be so impatient and hasty, and why she was not always compassionate in her judgment of others!

Gertrude was an excellent scholar, taking advantage of all that Helfta had to offer in the way of sacred and secular learning. In due course she became a professed nun of this large, happy and intellectu-ally stimulating community. However, her course had been like that of many who join religious life young. She had grown to maturity enjoying and adapting quickly to a monastic form of life, reveling in the accumulation of knowledge, but not truly committed to Christ because she had not made a personal choice of him. Without this personal choice of Christ one can be a religious in name and live an outwardly observant life, but there is no animating spirit to give direction to the emergent Christ-self, which must rise from the ashes of the ego.

Gertrude herself tells us that this changed when she was twenty-five. After a period during which she felt disturbed and ambivalent about the direction her life was taking, she underwent a profound conversion experience that divided her life into "before and after." The event which brought her to a personal encounter with Christ took place in the monastic dormitory one winter evening, where she realized for the first time the desirability of Christ and his invitation to greater intimacy. This encounter gradually changed her from her primary focus on secular learning to a more biblical and liturgically based theology which would nourish her emerging life of prayer.

As Benedictine nuns, Mechtild and Gertrude lived their whole lives in the ambience of a monastery, with its regular hours of chanting the Divine Office, with the rest of the time divided between private prayer, study and reading. Gertrude's love for her surroundings is especially evident in her beautiful description of the cloister garth where she went to pray one morning after Prime, and other references to her monastery and community. Most of her visions took place within the context of the liturgy, the annual circle of feasts and fasts that formed the backbone of regular monastic life. Gertrude did not have to go elsewhere to find the God she so eagerly sought. God was here with her in her daily life, among the sisters with whom she shared her insights, and with whom she celebrated the liturgy.

Gertrude was heavily influenced by the bridal mysticism of the period, which attributed to religious women, and especially those in monastic communities, the title "bride of Christ," but she is no mere sentimentalist. Her insights into the mystery of bridal love bore fruit in a life of sisterly charity, service, and a constant battle with her faults. Above all, her (and Mechtild's) devotion to the heart of Christ laid the foundations for an affective piety that had far-reaching consequences. The relationship of the soul to the transcendent God, such as described by Gertrude and founded on personal love for the wounded Savior, was to culminate in the devotion to the Sacred Heart that influenced the whole of Catholic piety in the time of Saint Margaret Mary Alacoque

(1647–1690). Gertrude does her best to communicate in similitudes and descriptive passages what it means to love God in such a way that one is totally transformed into the Beloved.

It is noteworthy that the virtue God is considered to have loved best in Gertrude was her "liberty of heart," or pure conscience. She was not troubled about whether she was thought to be the "perfect nun" or not. Her one desire was to please God, even to the extent of being thought hasty and impatient by some, as indeed she was!

Gertrude's work is generally included in one volume entitled *The Herald of Divine Love* which comprises three books. The first book is an account of her life and virtues and was compiled from anecdotes about her (drawing quite heavily on her friendship with Mechtild). The second book *The Memorial of the Abundance of Divine Sweetness* is considered to be from Gertrude's own hand, and in it there is much fine descriptive writing. Book three recounts further incidents from the saint's life which are accepted as authentic.

In choosing and arranging these texts I have used the volume in the Classics of Western Spirituality series, published by Paulist Press in 1993, translated and edited by Margaret Winkworth. On the whole I have followed the order of the Herald with a few exceptions, giving to each piece a title of my own and placing it in an appropriate setting. This means that the reader begins with some anecdotes relating to Gertrude's life and character. This is followed by extracts from Gertrude's own writings, beginning with her famous conversion experience. Lastly there are some passages from book three, nearly all related to Holy Communion which was a pivot of devotion for Gertrude's spiritual life and closely linked with her love of Christ's heart. I have chosen to end with Gertrude's own prayer of thanksgiving in which she recounts the graces of God as manifested in her life. The fact that she attributed all she had received to the grace and the love of Christ makes us realize how fully she acknowledged herself to be the recipient of love; and because she had received so much, much would be required of her in return.

Gertrude through the Eyes of Those Who Knew Her

Why the Lord chose to dwell in Gertrude

A man to whom she was entirely unknown except that she had recommended herself to his prayers, was praying for her and received this answer. "I have chosen to dwell in her because it delights me to see that everything that people love in her is my own work. Those who know nothing of interior, that is, spiritual, things, love in her at least my exterior gifts, such as intelligence, eloquence, and so on. Therefore I have exiled her from all relatives, so that there should be no one who would love her for the sake of ties of blood, and that I may be the only reason why all her friends love her."

(Book I:16)

Gertrude's freedom of heart

The freedom of her spirit was so great that she could not tolerate even for an instant anything that went against her conscience. The Lord himself bore witness to this, because when someone asked him in devout prayer what it was that pleased him most in his chosen one, he replied: "her freedom of heart." This person, most astonished and, so to speak, considering this an inadequate answer, said: "I should have thought, Lord, that by your grace she would have attained to a higher knowledge of your mysteries and a greater fervor of love." To which the Lord answered: "Yes, indeed, it is as you think. And this is the result of the grace of the freedom of her heart, which is so great a good that it leads directly to the highest perfection. I have always found her ready to receive my gifts, for she permits nothing to remain in her heart which might impede my action."

As a consequence of this great freedom, she could not bear to keep for her own use anything which was not indispensable, and if she accepted presents, she at once distributed them to others, taking care to give first to those who had most need, regardless of whether they were most loving or most hostile toward her.

(*Book* I:11)

Gertrude's joy in being generous with others

Her happiness was all the greater when she could give something to others, and then she was as happy as a miser who has received a hundred marks instead of a single little coin.

(*Book* I:11)

Gertrude's alacrity

If she had something to do or say she did it at once, lest it should hinder her in the service of God or in the work of contemplation. One day Dame Mechtild, our chantress, saw the Lord seated on a high throne. She of whom we write was walking up and down, coming and going before him, frequently turning to look at the face of the Lord and eagerly attending with most ardent desire to the aspirations of the divine heart. As Mechtild looked on in wonder, she received this response: "You see what the life of my chosen one is like. She is always in my presence, as though walking ceaselessly up and down. She ardently desires and seeks at every moment how to please my heart. As soon as she has found out what I want, she at once sets about busily to do my will, with all her heart; and when she has done what I wanted her to do, back she comes again to find out what is my further pleasure, and goes off to do it; in this way she gives her whole life faithfully to me in praise and honor." Then Mechtild said: "O my Lord, if her life is like that, how can it be that sometimes she judges with severity the excesses and defects of others?" To this the Lord replied kindly: "Certainly it is because she allows no spot to stain her own heart, and so she cannot tolerate with equanimity the defects of others."

(*Book* I:11)

Gertrude's natural impulsiveness

Dame Mechtild asked the Lord whether (Gertrude's) conduct were not perhaps rather reprehensible, because she always hastened to do whatever came into her head; and how it was all the same to her and no trouble to her conscience whether she prayed, read, wrote, gave instruction, corrected, or consoled others. The Lord replied: "I have deigned to join my heart so courteously and so inseparably with her soul that she has become one spirit with me and her will is always in perfect harmony with my own in all things and above all things, just as the members of the body are in harmony among themselves and with the will. When a man thinks in his mind and says to his hand: 'Do this,' at once the hand moves to perform the action. Again he says; 'Look at that,' and at once the eyes are opened without delay. Thus through my grace she is always intent on asking me what I want her to do. For I have chosen to dwell in her in such a way that her will, and the works which stem from this good will, are so firmly fixed in my heart that she is, as it were, the right hand with which I work. Her understanding is like my own eye with which she perceives what pleases me; the movement of her spirit is like my own tongue, since, inspired by the Spirit, she says what I intend to be said. And her discretion is like my nostrils for I incline the ears of my mercy toward those for whom she is moved to compassion. And her attention is like feet for me, because she is always bent on going where it is fitting for me to follow. Therefore it is necessary for her to be always hurrying, according to the promptings of my Spirit, so that as soon as she has finished one thing, she may be ready to begin another, at my bidding. And if in doing this she has to neglect something, her conscience is never troubled, because by doing my will she makes up for it in some other way."

(*Book* I:16)

Gertrude in Her Own Words

Gertrude's conversion

I was in my twenty-sixth year. The day of my salvation was the Monday preceding the feast of the Purification of your most chaste Mother, which fell that year on the 27th of January. The desirable hour was after Compline, as dusk was falling.

My God, you who are all truth, clearer than all light, yet hidden deeper in our heart than any secret, when you resolved to disperse the darkness of my night, you began gently and tenderly by first calming my mind, which had been troubled for more than a month past. This trouble, it seems to me, served your purpose. You were striving to destroy the tower of vanity and worldliness which I had set up in my pride, although, alas, I was—in vain—bearing the name and wearing the habit of a religious. This was the way in which you sought to show me your salvation.

At the stated hour, then, I was standing in the middle of the dormitory. An older nun was approaching and, having bowed my head with the reverence prescribed by our rule, I looked up and saw before me a youth of about sixteen years of age, handsome and gracious. Young as I then was, the beauty of his form was all that I could have desired, entirely pleasing to the outward eye. Courteously and in a gentle voice he said to me: "Soon will come your salvation; why are you so sad? Is it because you have no one to confide in that you are sorrowful?"

While he was speaking, although I knew that I was really in the place where I have said, it seemed to me that I was in the Choir, in the corner where I usually say my tepid prayers; and it was there that I heard these words: "I will save you. I will deliver you. Do not fear." With this, I saw his hand, tender and fine, holding mine, as though to plight a troth, and he added: "With my enemies you have licked the dust and sucked honey among thorns. Come back to me now, and I will inebriate you with the torrent of my divine pleasure."

As he was saying this, I looked and saw, between him and me, that is to say, on his right and on my left, a hedge of such length that I could not see the end of it, either ahead or behind. The top of this hedge was bristling with such large thorns that there seemed no way to get back to the youth. As I hesitated, burning with desire and almost fainting, suddenly he seized me and, lifting me up with the greatest ease, placed me beside him. But on the hand with which he had just given me his promise I recognized those bright jewels, his wounds, which have canceled all our debts.

I praise, adore, bless, and thank you to the best of my ability for your wise mercy and your merciful wisdom! For you, my Creator and my Redeemer, have sought to curb my stiff-necked obstinacy under your sweet yoke with the remedy best suited to my infirmity. From that hour, in a new spirit of joyful serenity, I began to follow the way of the sweet odor of your perfumes, and I found your yoke sweet and your burden light which a short time before I had thought to be unbearable.

(*Book* II:1)

God's indwelling in the soul

One day between Easter and Ascension I went into the garden before Prime, and, sitting down beside the pond, I began to consider what a pleasant place it was. I was charmed by the clear water and flowing streams, the fresh green of the surrounding trees, the birds flying so freely about, especially the doves. But most of all, I loved the quiet, hidden peace of this secluded retreat. I asked myself what more was needed to complete my happiness in a place that seemed to me so perfect, and I reflected that it was the presence of a friend, intimate, wise, affectionate, and companionable, to share my solitude.

And then you, my God, source of ineffable delights, who, as I believe, did but inspire the beginning of this meditation to lead it back to yourself, made me understand that, if I were to pour back like water the stream of graces received from you in that continual gratitude I owe you; if, like a tree, growing in the exercise of virtue, I were to cover myself with the leaves and blossoms of good works; if, like the doves, I were to spurn earth and soar heavenward; and if, with my senses set free from passions and worldly distractions, I were to occupy myself with you alone; then my heart would afford you a dwelling most suitably appointed from which no joys would be lacking.

I pondered these thoughts all day in my mind, and at evening, as I was kneeling in prayer before going to rest, suddenly there came into my head this passage from the gospel: "If anyone loves me, he will keep my word. And my Father will love him; and we will come to him and make our abode with him." And inwardly my heart of clay felt your coming and your presence.

(*Book* II:3)

Gertrude receives the wounds of Christ within her soul

At the time when I first began to receive these favors—I think it was during the first or the second year, in the winter—I found in a book a short prayer in these words:

Lord Jesus Christ, Son of the living God,
grant that I may, with all my heart,
all my desire,
and with a thirsting soul,
aspire toward you;
and in you, most sweet and pleasant, take my rest.
With my whole spirit and all that is within me,
may I sigh always for you
in whom alone true blessedness is to be found.
Inscribe with your precious blood, most merciful Lord,

your wounds in my heart,
that I may read in them both your sufferings and your love.
May the memory of your wounds
ever remain in the hidden places of my heart,
to stir up within me your compassionate sorrow,
so that the flame of your love may be enkindled in me.
Grant also that all creatures may become vile to me,
and that you may become the only sweetness of my heart.

I was so pleased with this little prayer that I repeated it often with great fervor; and you, who never refuse to grant the requests of the humble, were to grant me the effects of the prayer. . . .

While I was devoutly meditating on these things, I felt, in my extreme unworthiness, that I had received supernaturally the favors for which I had been asking in the words of the prayer I spoke of. I knew in my spirit that I had received the stigmata of your adorable and venerable wounds interiorly in my heart, just as though they had been made on the natural places of the body. By these wounds you not only healed my soul, but you gave me to drink of the inebriating cup of love's nectar. Even so, unworthy as I am, I found that the depths of your love was not exhausted. Did I not receive of the overflowing of your generous love another remarkable gift? On any one day that I recited five verses of the psalm "Bless the Lord, O my soul" (psalm 102) while venerating in my spirit the marks of your love impressed on my heart, I cannot claim that I was ever denied some special grace. . . .

In this way you granted the petition of my prayer, the grace to read in these wounds your suffering and your love. It was, alas, for a short time only. I do not claim that you withdrew these favors from me, but my complaint is that I lost them myself through my own ingratitude and negligence. In your infinite mercy and love, you seemed not to notice this. Up to the present time you have preserved your first and greatest gift, the impression of your wounds, although most unworthy as I am, I did nothing to deserve it.

May glory, honor, and power with joyful praise be given to you in all eternity!

(*Book* II:4)

Meditating on the Crucified

After I had received the life-giving sacrament, on returning to my place, it seemed to me as if, on the right side of the Crucified painted in the book, that is to say, on the wound in the side, a ray of sunlight with a sharp point like an arrow came forth and spread itself out for a moment and then drew back. Then it spread out again. It continued like this for a while and affected me gently but deeply. But even so my desire was not fully satisfied until the Wednesday when, after Mass, the faithful venerate the mystery of your adorable Incarnation and Annunciation. I too tried to apply myself to this devotion, but less worthily. Suddenly you appeared, inflicting a wound in my heart, and saying: "May all the affections of your heart be concentrated here: all pleasure, hope, joy, sorrow, fear, and the rest; may they all be fixed in my love."

At once it occurred to me that I had heard it said that wounds have to be bathed, anointed and bandaged. You had not taught me then how to do this, but afterward you showed me through another person. She was more accustomed, I believe, to listen more frequently and consistently, for the sake of your glory, to the soft murmur of your love than was I, alas. She now advised me to meditate devoutly on the love of your heart as you hung on the cross, so that from the fountains of charity flowing from the fervor of such inestimable love, I might derive the oil of gratitude, balm against all adversity; and in efficacious charity perfected by the strength of such incomprehensible love, I might derive the bandage of holiness, so that all my thoughts, words and deeds, in the strength of your love, might be turned toward you and thus cleave indissolubly to you.

(*Book* II:5)

Vision at Christmas

While still on my earthly pilgrimage, I want to recapture what I can of the prelude to the delectable bliss and sweetest delights of that state in which a soul united with God becomes one spirit with him. It has been given to me, poor little speck of dust that I am, to dare to lap up some of the drops of this infinite beatitude, overflowing so abundantly in the way I am about to relate.

It was in the holy night, when the dew of divinity came down, shedding sweetness over all the earth, and the heavens were melting, made sweet like honey. My soul, like a dampened fleece on the threshing floor of the community, was meditating on this mystery. Through the exercise of this devotion, I was trying to give my poor services in assisting at the divine birth when, like a star shedding its ray, the Virgin brought forth her son, true God and true man. In an instant I knew what it was that I was being offered and what it was that I received, as it were, into the heart of my soul: a tender newborn babe. In him was hidden the supreme gift of perfection, truly the very best of gifts. And while I held him within my soul, suddenly I saw myself entirely transformed into the color of the heavenly babe—if it were possible to describe as color that which cannot be compared with any visible form. Then I received into my soul intelligence of those sweetest and most ineffable words: "God shall be all in all." I rejoiced that I was not denied the welcome presence and delightful caresses of my Spouse. With insatiable avidity, therefore, I drank in, like deep draughts from a cup of nectar, divinely inspired words such as these: "As I am the figure of the substance of the Father through my divine nature, in the same way, you shall be the figure of my substance through my human nature, receiving in your deified soul the brightness of my divinity, as the air receives the sun's rays and, penetrated to the very narrow by this unifying light, you will become capable of an ever closer union with me."

. . . Oh, what invincible power is shown in the right hand of the Most High, that such a fragile vessel of clay as mine, cast into ignominy through her own defects, should hold and keep a liquid so precious.

(*Book* II:6)

Gertrude's heart imprinted with the seal of Christ

On the most holy feast of the Purification, after a serious illness, I was obliged to stay in bed. Toward daybreak I was filled with sadness. I complained within myself of being deprived, through bodily infirmity, of that divine visitation which had so often consoled me on this feast day. She who is our mediatrix, the mother of him who is the mediator between God and humankind, comforted me with these words: "Just as you do not remember ever having suffered any greater bodily pain, know that you have never received from my son a nobler gift than the one which this bodily weakness has given your soul the strength to receive worthily." These words consoled me, and just before the procession was due to start, after I had received the food of life and as I was meditating on God and myself, I saw my soul, like wax melting in the heat of the fire, being placed close to the Lord's most sacred breast, as though to take the imprint of a seal. Suddenly, as I looked, it seemed to be spread around and even to be drawn into the interior of that treasury wherein all the fullness of the Godhead corporeally dwells. Thus it was sealed with the imprint of the resplendent and ever tranquil Trinity. . . .

The Lord appeared to me, and I saw that that part of his sacred breast to which he had taken my soul on the day of the Purification and held it like wax being carefully melted in the fire was now moist with perspiration and breaking out violently in beads of sweat, as though the wax of which I had formerly had sight were melting in the intense heat of the hidden fire which was burning there. And yet this divine treasury, with marvelous and ineffable power, absorbed these drops in an indescribable way. Who could doubt the mighty power of the boundless love stored up therein, disclosing a mystery so great and so unfathomable?

O eternal solstice, happy fields where joy securely dwells, containing all manner of delights, paradise of bliss that never cloys, where flows a stream of inestimable pleasure! Blossoms and spring flowers of every kind and hue gladden the sight; one is moved softly by sweet harmonies, sweetly influenced, rather, by the melodies of the spiritual songs and music; revived by the aromatic odors of life-enhancing perfumes; intoxicated by sweet savors interiorly tasted; one is wonderfully changed by gentle and secret embraces!

Oh, thrice happy, four times blessed and (if it may be said) a hundred times holy he who, with innocent hands, a pure heart, and unpolluted lips, led by your grace, has deserved to approach this paradise! Oh, what will he not see, hear, smell, taste, feel! But even if my tongue were to stammer out something from thence, I who have been admitted, favored by divine goodness, if only by way of my own vices and negligences, as though all covered with a thick crust, I should never really be able to grasp any of it. Although the knowledge of angels and human beings were to be worthily combined, even that would not suffice to form one single word that might accurately express even a shadow of such sovereign excellence.

(*Book* II:7, 8)

Temptation and spiritual growth

Once when I was assisting at Mass during which I was to go to communion, you let me feel your presence; and with wonderful humility, you instructed me with this similitude: I saw that you were thirsty and asking me to give you a drink. As I was lamenting my inability to help you, because, in spite of all my efforts, I was unable to wring from my heart a single tear, I saw that you were offering me a golden cup. As soon as I had taken it, my heart melted with tenderness and a flood of loving tears gushed forth. Meanwhile a contemptible figure had appeared on my left, stealthily placing in my hand something bitter and poisonous, trying without being seen but with all his might to make me throw it into the cup to pollute it. At that very instant there arose in me such a vehement temptation to vainglory that it was easy to see in it a device of our old adversary, jealous of your gifts to us.

But thanks to your faithfulness Lord, thanks to your protection, truly one Divinity, one and threefold Truth, threefold and one Godhead, you do not allow us to be tempted beyond our powers. Although you sometimes give the enemy the power to tempt us, in order to exercise us in spiritual progress, if you see that we continue to strive confidently, trusting in your help, you make the strife your own; in your boundless generosity you keep the battle for yourself, and attribute the victory to us, if only we cleave to you of our own free will; and among all your gifts this one in particular is always preserved for us by your grace, to increase our merits. Not only do you never allow our enemy to take our free will from us, but you never have the slightest wish to take it from us yourself.

On another occasion and by another similitude, you taught me that by giving in easily to the adversary we allow him to grow in audacity, for the perfect beauty of your justice requires your merciful power to be hidden sometimes during the dangers we incur through our own negligence. The more promptly we resist evil, the more profitable, fruitful, and successful is our resistance.

(*Book* II:11)

Christ remains with us even when we sin

One evening I had given way to anger, and the next day, before dawn, I was taking the first opportunity to pray when you showed yourself to me in the form and guise of a pilgrim; as far as I could judge, you seemed to be destitute and helpless. Filled with remorse, with a guilty conscience, I bewailed my lapse of the previous day. I began to consider how unseemly it was to disturb you, Author of perfect purity and peace, with the turmoil of our wicked passions, and I thought it would be better—rather, I considered that I would actually prefer—to have you absent rather than present (but at such a time only) when I neglected to repel the enemy who was inciting me to do things so contrary to your nature.

This was your reply: "What consolation would there be for a sick person who, leaning on others, has just succeeded in going out to enjoy the sunshine when he is suddenly overtaken by a storm, had he not the hope of seeing the clear sky again? In the same way, overcome by my love for you I have chosen to remain with you during the storm brought on by your sins and to await the clear sky of your amendment in the shelter of your humiliation."

(*Book* II:12)

Suffering and works of charity add brilliance to the soul

When the body is afflicted and touched by suffering, it is as though the soul were bathed in air and sunlight, which comes to it through the suffering member, and this imparts to it a marvelous clarity. The more intense the pain, or the more general the suffering, the more the soul is purified and clarified. This is especially true of afflictions and trials of the heart. When these are borne with humility, patience, and other virtues, they lend a wonderful luster to the soul, the nearer, the more effective, and the closer they touch it. But it is works of charity above all that cause it to shine with a pure brilliance.

(*Book* II:15)

The mystery of Divine Forbearance

One day after washing my hands I was waiting with the community in the cloisters before going into the refectory, when

I noticed the brightness of the sun, shining at the height of its noonday strength. Marveling, I said to myself: "If the Lord who created the sun, the Lord of whom it is said that the sun and moon admire his beauty, and who is himself a consuming fire, is really united with my soul in the way in which he so often reveals himself to me, how is it that I can treat my companions so coldly, so discourteously and even wickedly?" And suddenly you, whose speech is always sweet, but was then the sweeter the more my vacillating heart had need of it, led me to infer this saying: "How would my infinite power be extolled if I did not reserve to myself the power, in whatever place I might be, of keeping myself to myself, so that I might make myself felt or seen only in the way that is most fitting according to places, times, and persons? For from the beginning of the creation of heaven and earth, and in the whole work of the Redemption, I have employed wisdom and goodness rather than power and majesty. And the goodness of this wisdom shines forth best in my bearing with imperfect creatures till I draw them, of their own free will, into the way of perfection."

(Book II:17)

Image of the father and his child

In your fatherly love you told me that I should regard your affection for me like that of a father who takes pleasure in hearing his large family of children complimented by retainers and friends for their elegance and grace. This father has a small child also, who has not yet attained to the elegance and perfection of the others, but for whom he feels a compassionate tenderness, pressing him more often to his breast, fondling and caressing him with more endearing words and little gifts than he gives to the others. You added that if I really believed that I was the least and most imperfect of all, then a torrent of your honey-sweet divinity would always continue to flow into my soul.

(Book II:18)

The divine gaze

On the second Sunday of Lent, before Mass, as the procession was about to start and they were singing the Response "I saw the Lord face to face," my soul was suddenly illumined by a flash of indescribable and marvelous brightness. In the light of this divine revelation there appeared to me a Face as though close to my face, as Bernard says: "Unformed but forming everything, it touches not the eye of the body but rejoices the face of the heart, and charms not by any visible color but with the radiance of love." In this sweetest vision in which your eyes, shining like the sun, seemed to be gazing straight into mine, how you, my dearest and sweetest, touched not only my soul but my heart and every limb, is known to you alone and as long as I live I shall be your devoted slave.

Although a rose in spring, when it is fresh, blooming, and fragrant, is more pleasing by far than one found in winter when, long since withered, its sweet scent is evoked in words, yet the latter can to some extent revive the memory of former loveliness. And so I want, if I can, in my nothingness, to find some similitude to describe what I felt in that most blissful vision of you, in praise of your love. Then perhaps some reader, having received a similar or even greater grace, may be reminded to give thanks. And I myself, by often recalling it, may disperse somewhat the darkness of my negligences through the rays of my gratitude reflected in this mirror.

When you showed me your most longed-for face, full of blessedness, as I have just said, so close to mine (though I am so undeserving), I felt as though an ineffable light from your divine eyes were entering through my eyes, softly penetrating, passing through all my interior being, in a way wonderful beyond measure, working with marvelous power in every limb. At first it was as though my bones were being emptied of all the marrow, then even the bones with the flesh were dissolved so that nothing was felt to exist in all my substance save that divine splendor which, in a manner more delectable than I am able to say, playing within itself, showed my soul the inestimable bliss of utter serenity.

(*Book* II:21)

Further Teaching of Gertrude Recorded by a Companion

The soul's cooperation with God

On the feast of St. Maurice while Mass was being celebrated and the priest was proceeding to the silent words of the consecration of the host, she said to the Lord: "This act, Lord, that you are about to perform deserves a perfect and infinite respect; and that is why I, who am so insignificant, dare not even raise my eyes to it. Rather, I shall plunge myself down and lie in the deepest valley of humility I can find, there to await my portion of it; for from it comes the salvation of all the elect."

To which the Lord answered: "When a mother wants to do some embroidery with silk or pearls, sometimes she puts her little one in a higher place to hold the thread of pearls or help her in some other way. And so I have put you in a higher place with the intention of making you participate in this Mass. Because, if you will raise yourself up to help me of your own free will in this work, even if it is hard; if you want to be of service so that this oblation may have its full effect on all Christians, whether living or dead, in accordance with its dignity and excellence; then you will have given me the best possible help in my work, according to your possibilities."

(*Book* III:6)

A tree planted in the side of Christ

Another day, when she was going to participate in the divine mysteries, while she was recalling God's goodness to her, there came into her mind this quotation from the book of Kings: "Who am I or what is the house of my father?" (1 Sam. 18:18). Rejecting the words "the house of my father," since she assumed that her ancestors had been people who had lived their lives according to the law of God, she considered herself, a frail little plant, placed close to the inextinguishable furnace of the divine heart, receiving the benefit of its warmth, burning within herself as if naturally, yet fading away from hour to hour through her faults and negligence till at length she was brought almost to nothing, lying there like the smallest of burned-out coals. Turning then to Jesus, the Son of God, her loving Mediator, she prayed that he would deign to present her, just as she was, to be reconciled to God the Father. Her most loving Jesus seemed to draw her toward himself by the breath of love of his pierced heart, and to wash her in the water flowing from it, and then to sprinkle her with the life-giving blood of his heart. With this action she began to revive, and from the smallest cinder she was invigorated and grew into a green tree, whose branches were divided in three, in the form of a fleur-de-lys. Then the Son of God took this tree and presented it with gratitude to the glory of the ever adorable Trinity. When he had presented it, the whole blessed Trinity with great graciousness bowed down toward the offering. God the Father, in his divine omnipotence, set in the upper branches all the fruit that this soul would have been able to produce, were she to correspond aright to divine omnipotence. In the same way, she saw the Son of God and the Holy Spirit setting in the other two sections of the branches the fruits of wisdom and goodness.

Afterward, when she had received the body of Christ, she beheld her soul, as was said above, in the likeness of a tree fixing its roots in the wound of the side of Jesus Christ; she felt in some new and marvelous way that there was passing through this wound, as through a root, and penetrating into all her branches and fruit and leaves a wondrous sap which was the virtue of the humanity and divinity of Jesus Christ. Thus, through her soul, the work of his whole life took on more splendor, like gold gleaming through crystal. Hereupon not only the blessed Trinity, but all the saints, rejoiced with delight and wonder. They all rose up in reverence and, as though on bended knee, offered their merits, represented like crowns, hanging them on the branches of the tree we have mentioned, to the praise and honor of him, the splendor of whose glory now shone through her and gladdened them with fresh delight. As for her, she besought the Lord that all those in heaven and on earth and even in purgatory (for indeed, all would have benefitted from the fruits of her works, had she not been negligent) might now have at least some share in those fruits with which she had just been enriched by his divine generosity. As she was praying, each single one of her good works (symbolized by the fruits of the tree) began to distill a beneficent liquid. Part of this liquid spread over the blessed, increasing their bliss; part of it spread out over purgatory, easing the pain of souls; another part of it spread over the earth, increasing the sweetness of grace for the just, and for sinners the bitterness of repentance.

(*Book* III:18)

On sins of the tongue

One day, after having received communion, she was meditating on the care with which we should watch over the tongue, since it is the tongue more than all other members of the body which receives the most precious mystery of Christ. She was instructed by this comparison: that anyone who does not restrain his tongue from uttering vain words, false, shameful, slanderous words and the like, and goes unrepentant to communion, receives Christ (as far as he can do so) as if he were receiving a guest by pelting him on arrival with the stones that were heaped around the door, or by dealing him a blow on the head with a heavy bar. Let anyone who reads these lines ponder then with tears of deep compassion, considering how so much kindness can be met with so many injuries, and how he who came with gentleness for the salvation of humanity can be so cruelly treated by the very ones he came to save. The same could be said of any other sin.

(*Book* III:18)

The Lord who is as a pelican feeding its young

She had received communion and while recollecting herself, the Lord showed himself to her in the form of a pelican, such as is usually represented, piercing its heart with its beak. Looking at it in wonder, she said: "O my Lord, what are you trying to teach me by this similitude?" The Lord replied: "That you may consider what ineffable ardor of love compels me to offer such a precious gift; and if it does not sound too paradoxical to say this, that I should prefer that this gift would lead to my death, rather than that I should deprive a loving soul of this gift of myself. Moreover, you must consider the excellent way in which your soul, in receiving this gift, is invigorated and receives the life which lasts eternally; just as the little pelican is invigorated with the blood from the father's heart."

(*Book* III:18)

The two wounds and the sacred host

On another day before communion she abased herself according to her frequent custom on account of her unworthiness, imploring the Lord to receive his most sacred host for her himself in his own person in her place and to incorporate it into himself; and then to breathe into her each hour with his sweet and noble breath just as much as he knew to be suitable to her small capacity. After that, she reposed for a time in the bosom of the Lord, as it were beneath the shadow of his arm. She was so placed that her left side seemed to be held against the Lord's blessed right side. After a little while, raising herself, she perceived that through the contact with the wound of love in the

Lord's most sacred side, her left side had been drawn into a sort of ruddy scar. Then, as she was going to receive the body of Christ, the Lord himself seemed to receive the consecrated host in his divine mouth. It passed through his body and proceeded to issue from the wound in the most sacred side of Christ, and to fix itself almost like a dressing over the life-giving wound. And the Lord said to her: "Behold, this host will unite you to me in such a way that on one side it touches your scar and on the other my wound, like a dressing for both of us. You must cleanse it as it were, and renew it every day by turning over in your mind with devotion the hymn *'Jesu nostra redemptio.'* " After this it pleased him, as if to show the growing intensity of her desire, to increase this practice of piety every day; so that one day she recited the hymn once, the second day twice, and the third day three times, and so on until the day when next she was to go to communion.

(*Book* III:18)

Mary, Lily of the Trinity

It was the hour of prayer and, coming into the presence of God, she asked him what subject he would most like to apply herself to during that hour. The Lord answered: "Keep close to my mother who is seated at my side, and strive to praise her."

. . . After a little time had passed, Gertrude said to the Lord: "O my brother, since you were made man to make up for all human defects, now deign to make up to your blessed Mother for what may have been lacking in my praise of her." When he heard these words, the Son of God arose and most reverently went to kneel before his Mother; bowing his head, he saluted her most courteously and affectionately, so that she could not but be pleased with the homage of one whose imperfections were so abundantly made up for by her beloved Son.

The following day, as she was praying in this way, the Virgin Mother appeared to her in the presence of the ever adorable Trinity, which appeared in the form of a fleur-de-lys, as it is usually shown with three petals, one erect and two turning downward. Thus she was given to understand that the blessed Mother of God is justly called the White Lily of the Trinity, because she has received into herself, more fully and perfectly than any other creature, the virtues of the adorable Trinity; virtues which she never stained with even the least speck of venial sin. The erect petal denotes the omnipotence of God the Father; the two turning downward, the Wisdom and Love of the Son and the Holy Spirit, whom she most resembles. Wherefore she understood from the blessed Virgin that if one were to salute her devoutly with the words: "White Lily of the Trinity and fairest Rose of heavenly bliss," she would show how great is her power through the omnipotence of the Father; and with what ingenuity she knows how to work for the salvation of the human race, through the wisdom of the Son; and how immeasurably her heart abounds in tenderness, through the love of the Holy Spirit. . . .

From that time Gertrude resolved to salute the blessed Virgin, or her images, with these words: "Hail, White Lily of the resplendent and ever tranquil Trinity! Fairest Rose of heavenly bliss! The King of heaven chose to be born of you, to be fed with your milk! Oh, feed our souls on the outpourings of divine grace!"

(*Book* III:19)

The cloister of the Lord's body

At Vespers, while they were singing *"Vidi aquam egredientem"* the Lord said to her: "Behold my heart; now it will be your temple. And now look among the other parts of my body and choose for yourself other places in which you can lead a monastic life, because from now on my body will be your cloister." To this she said: "Lord, I do not know how to seek further or how to choose, because I find such sweet plenty in your sweetest heart, which you deign to call my temple, that apart from it I am unable to find any rest or refreshment, both of which are necessary in a cloister." Then the Lord said: "If it pleases you, you may find both these things in my heart; for you have heard about others who, like [Saint] Dominic, never left the temple, eating and even sleeping there. Do choose, however, some other place which you think would be expedient to have in your cloister."

Then, at the Lord's bidding, she chose the Lord's feet for a hall or ambulatory; his hands for workshop; his mouth for parlor and chapter house; his eyes for library where she might read; and his ears for confessional. Then the Lord taught her that she should always go up to it after each fall, as though ascending the five steps of humiliation, which are to be remembered by these five expressions; "I, a wretch, a sinner, a beggar, evil, unworthy, come to you as to the overflowing abyss of mercy, to be washed from every stain and to be cleansed from every sin. Amen."

(*Book* III:28)

We receive what we truly desire

Carried away by her love, she said to the Lord one day: "How I wish, O Lord, that my soul might burn with such a fire that it might melt and be like some liquid substance, so that it could be entirely poured out into you!" He answered: "Your will is to you such a fire." By these words she saw that it is by his will that a man receives the full effect of all the desires he has as regards God.

(*Book* III:30)

Feeling depressed

One day she was feeling depressed about some little matter of no importance. At the elevation of the host she offered this feeling of desolation to God's eternal praise. Then the Lord seemed to attract her soul through the most sacred host as though through a gateway and, making her rest sweetly on his bosom, he tenderly spoke these words: "See, in this resting place you will breathe free from all troubles, but every time you leave it, bitterness will invade your heart again, and this will be a saving antidote."

(*Book* III:30)

Feeling worn out

On another occasion she was feeling worn out and said to the Lord: "O my Lord, what is to become of me? What do you want of me?" The Lord answered: "As a mother comforts her child, I will comfort you." He added: "Haven't you ever seen a mother caressing her child?" At this, she was silent, not being able to remember. The Lord recalled to her mind that scarcely six months before she had seen a mother fondling her little child, and he reminded her especially of three things she had not noticed at that time. First, the mother often asked her little child to kiss her, at which the little one was obliged to raise himself with an effort on his weak little legs. The Lord added that it was necessary to raise oneself with a great effort by means of contemplation to the enjoyment of the sweetness of his love. Second, the mother tested the will of her child, saying: "Do you want this? Do you want this or that?" and let him have nothing. So God tries a man when he makes him foresee great troubles which never come to anything. However, when a man submits willingly, God is fully satisfied and makes him worthy of an eternal reward. Third, when the child spoke, no one present could understand a word the little boy said, save only his mother. So only God can understand man's intention and judges accordingly, far otherwise than man, who sees only exterior things.

(*Book* III:30)

Feeling downcast

Another time, when she was downcast at the memory of her former sins to such an extent that she desired only to hide herself completely, the Lord deigned to incline with such gracious condescension toward her that the whole court of heaven seemed to be trying to restrain him in astonishment. The Lord responded thus: "Nothing can restrain me from following her when she so powerfully attracts my heart by the cords of her humility."

(*Book* III:30)

The eyes of Christ prepare the soul for communion

When she came to Mass, very weak and longing for spiritual communion, it happened that a priest who had taken the body of Christ to a sick person was returning from the village. At the sound of the bell, she was filled with desire and said to the Lord: "Oh, how gladly would I receive you now, life of my soul, at least spiritually, had I but a little time in which to prepare myself!" He replied: "The eyes of my divine love will prepare you most fittingly." Upon which she saw the Lord looking at her, directing rays of sunlight into her soul and saying "I will fix my eyes on thee" (Ps. 31:8). By these words she understood that three things were effected in the soul by the divine gaze, which was like the sun, and that there were three ways in which the soul should prepare to receive them.

First, the look of divine love, like the sun, takes away all stains from the soul, purifying it and making it whiter than snow. And this effect can be gained by the recognition of one's own defects. Second, the look of divine love melts the soul and fits it to receive spiritual gifts, just as wax is melted by the sun's heat and made ready to take the imprint of the seal. And this effect the soul obtains by devout intentions. Third, the look of divine love makes the soul fruitful, so as to bring forth flowers of virtue, just as the sun gives fecundity to the earth so as to bring forth and multiply its various fruits. And this effect is obtained by faithful trust; for if a person abandons himself wholly to God, faithfully trusting in God's boundless love, everything, whether in adversity or in prosperity, will work together unto good.

(*Book* III:38)

Looking at the crucifix

One Friday, as evening was falling, she was looking at a crucifix. Moved to compunction, she said to the Lord: "Ah, my sweetest Lover, how many and how cruel sufferings you endured this day for my salvation, and I, alas, in my infidelity have made so little of it that I have passed this day occupied with other matters; I have not spent this day calling to mind with devotion what you, my eternal salvation, suffered for me at each hour, and that you, who are life itself and give life to all things, died for love of me!"

The Lord replied to her from the cross: "That which you were neglecting, I myself have supplied for you. For instance, every hour I gathered into my heart what you should have been recollecting in your heart, and afterward my heart was exceedingly full. Almost bursting with great desire, I have longed for this hour when you would make this intention your own. Now, with that intention of yours, I want to offer to God my Father all that which I have supplied for you throughout this day, for without your intention my action could not be so conducive to your salvation."

In this can be seen how very faithful is the love of God for humankind. In return for this single intention, whereby a man recognizes and is sorry for what he has neglected, the Lord makes amends to God the Father, and supplies fully, in the highest degree, for every defect, for which it is right that everyone should praise him.

Again, as she was holding a crucifix in her hand with devout attention, she was given to understand that if anyone were to look with a similar devout attention at an image of the crucified

Christ, the Lord would look at them with such benign mercy that their soul, like a burnished mirror, would reflect, by the effect of divine love, such a delectable image, that it would gladden the whole court of heaven. And as often as anyone does this on earth with affection and due devotion, it will be to his eternal glory in the future.

Another time she received this instruction. That when a person turns toward a crucifix, he is to consider in his heart that the Lord Jesus is saying to him in gentle tones: "See how I hung upon the cross for love of you, naked and despised, my body covered with wounds and every limb pulled out of joint. And now my heart is moved with such sweet charity toward you that, if it were expedient for your salvation, and if you could be saved in no other way, I would bear for you alone all that you may imagine I bore for the whole world." By such meditations the heart is incited to gratitude, because truly one cannot look at a crucifix without being touched by God's grace. Therefore a Christian so lacking in gratitude as to underestimate the immense price of his salvation could not be considered blameless; for never can one devoutly look upon a crucifix without receiving some fruit.

(*Book* III:41)

Contentment with God's will

Once she was ill with a fever, and sometimes after she had been perspiring profusely the fever increased, while sometimes it decreased. One night, bathed in perspiration, she began to wonder with some anxiety whether her sickness would take a turn for the worse or for the better. The Lord Jesus appeared to her, lovely as a flower; in his right hand he held health, and in his left hand sickness. He held out both hands to her at once so she might choose whichever she preferred. She, however, pushed them both aside and, making her way in the fervor of her spirit, she passed between the two outstretched hands of the Lord to reach his most sweet heart, where she knew that the plenitude of all good things is hidden, seeking only his adorable will, worthy of all praise. The

Lord received her tenderly and gently enfolded her in his embrace; she reclined for a while on his heart. Then, with her face turned away from the Lord and the back of her head still leaning on his breast, she said: "See, Lord, I turn my face away from you, desiring with all my heart that you pay no heed to my will, but that in all that concerns me, your adorable will be done."

By this let it be seen that a faithful soul commits herself and everything that is hers entirely and with such secure trust to the divine will that she actually delights in her ignorance of what the Lord may do in her regard, so that the divine will may be more purely and perfectly accomplished in her.

(Book III:53)

Why Gertrude's book was written

After this the Lord gave her to understand that it was his will that the story of these graces should be put down in writing for others to read. She asked herself wonderingly what good there could be in this; for in her heart she had firmly decided that she would never permit any of it to be known during her lifetime, and it seemed to her that if it were published after her death it would only cause trouble by disturbing the minds of the faithful, who would realize that they could now derive no profit from it. The Lord answered her thoughts thus: "And what good do you think it does to read that when I visited blessed Catherine [of Alexandria] in her prison I say to her: 'Be of good cheer, daughter, for I am with you!' Or when I called my special apostle John and said: 'Come to me, my beloved!' Or the many other things which one reads of these and of others? Is it not that devotion be increased in this way, serving as a reminder of my love for human beings?" And the Lord added: "When they hear about these graces that you have received, others may be brought to desire them for themselves, and by thinking about them, they may try somewhat to amend their lives."

(Book I:15)

Gertrude's Own Hymn of Thanksgiving

A paean of praise

May my soul bless you, Lord God my creator! May my soul bless you and, out of the very marrow of my inmost being, let me proclaim the mercies of the overflowing love with which you enfold me, O my sweetest lover!

I thank you as best I can for your great mercy, and I praise and bless the long-suffering patience which has led you to overlook all the years of my infancy and childhood, my girlhood and youth. Almost up to the end of my twenty-fifth year, in fact, in my blindness and stupidity it seems to me that I would have felt no remorse in following my instincts in all places and in everything—thoughts, words, and deeds—had you not prevented me from doing so, both by giving me an inborn loathing for evil and delight in well-doing, and by the correction and guidance of other people. And so I should have lived, like a pagan among pagans, without ever realizing that you, my God, reward good and punish evil. And yet, from my infancy, in my fifth year to be precise, you chose me to be formed among the most faithful of your friends, to live in the household of your holy religion. . . .

Again, I give you thanks, plunging myself into the profoundest abyss of humility. I praise and adore at the same time the supreme excellence of your mercy together with the sweet goodness by which, Father of mercies, while I was still leading my life of perdition you were thinking of me, thoughts of peace and not of affliction. You were lifting me up by the multitude and magnitude of your gifts, as though I were better than any other mortal, and my life on earth had been one of angelic innocence.

I began to feel the effects of this benevolence in the Advent preceding my twenty-fifth birthday, which took place on the following Epiphany. My heart began then to be agitated by some sort of trouble which gave me a great distaste for all the pursuits of my youth. This was the way you were preparing me to receive you in my heart. My twenty-sixth year, then, had already begun when, on the Monday before the feast of the Purification, after Compline, as dusk was falling, in the night of the trouble I have mentioned, you, the true light shining in darkness, put an end also to the day of my girlish vanity, obscured and darkened by my spiritual ignorance. For in that hour, with manifest condescension, and in a most delightful way, you approached me. With the greatest friendliness you reconciled me with yourself, making your presence known to me and teaching me to know something of your love; leading me to enter into my interior which before that time had been quite unknown to me. Then you began to deal with me in a marvelous and secret way. Like a friend in the house of a friend, or rather, like a spouse with his bride, you would always take pleasure in my soul. . . .

All that I have read or heard about the temple of Solomon or the palace of Ahasuerus could not be compared, I think, with the delights you have prepared for yourself in my heart, as I know by your grace, These, in spite of my unworthiness, you have given me the grace to share on equal terms, like a queen with a king.

Among these favors there were two which I shall mention in particular. They are the seal put on my heart with those brilliant jewels which are your salvific wounds, and the wound of love with which you so manifestly and efficaciously transfixed my heart. Had you given me no other consolation, interior or exterior, these two gifts alone would have held so much happiness that, were I to live a thousand years, I could never exhaust the fund of consolation, learning, and feelings of gratitude that I should derive from them at each hour.

In addition to these favors, you have granted me the priceless grace of your familiar friendship, giving me in various ways, to my indescribable delight, the noblest treasures of the divinity, your divine heart, now bestowing it freely, now as a sign of our mutual familiarity, exchanging it with mine. How often have you revealed to me your secret counsels and your pleasures, melting my soul with your loving caresses! Did I not know the abyss of your overflowing goodness, I wonder whether I should understand how you show such tokens as these marks of your lavish affection even on the creature of all others most worthy of them, your blessed Mother who reigns with you in heaven.

Sometimes you have led me to a salutary recognition of my faults, and you were as careful then to spare my blushes, as if—would it be wrong to say so?—it would be like losing half your kingdom were you to provoke my childish shame even a little. Also, by an ingenious device you showed me in others the faults which were displeasing to you. Rounding on myself, I found that I was even more guilty of the same faults than those other persons whom you had pointed out to me. But you never gave me the least indication that you found in me any trace of these defects.

You enticed my soul with your faithful promises, showing me the benefits you were ready to confer on me at death and after my death, so that, had I never had any other gifts from you, for this hope alone my soul would never cease to desire you with ardor. And still the ocean of your boundless love is not exhausted. For you constantly grant my prayers, whether for sinners, for souls, or for other intentions, answering them with incredible benefits. I have never found a human friend to whom I would dare tell all I know; the human heart is too small to bear it.

To all these other benefits you have added a crowning one in giving me your dearest mother, the most blessed Virgin Mary, to take care of me, commending me to her affection as often as a bridegroom commends his dearly beloved bride to his mother. . . .

More than all these favors and in a marvelous way, much to be preferred to all others, several times, particularly on the feast of the holy Nativity, and one Sunday (it was the Sunday of *Esto mihi*) and another Sunday after Pentecost, I was introduced by you—rapt rather—into so close a union with yourself that it seems more than miraculous that, after hours of ecstasy, I should still live as a mortal among mortals. What is really amazing, horrible rather, is that I have not amended my faults as it was just and right that I should do.

But none of this could dry up the fount of your mercy, O Jesus, most loving of all lovers, the only one whose love is sincere, free, and lavished on the undeserving.

Now, as time passed, most wretched, unworthy and ungrateful of creatures that I am, I began to lose the taste for these graces which should make heaven and earth continually dance for joy, rejoicing that you, from your infinite height, should graciously descend to my extreme lowness; you, O Giver, Renewer, and Preserver of all good things, aroused me from my torpor and revived my gratitude. And this you did by revealing the secret of your gifts to several persons whom I knew to be particularly faithful friends of yours. I am perfectly certain that they could have had it from no human source, for I revealed it to no one. And yet I heard it from their lips in words which I recognized secretly in my heart.

With these words, and all the others which now crowd into my mind, I want to render that which is your due. With the sweet melodious harp of your divine heart, through the power of the Holy Spirit, the Paraclete, I sing to you, Lord God, adorable Father, songs of praise and thanksgiving on behalf of all creatures in heaven, on earth, and under the earth; all which are, were, and shall be. . . .

You see into my heart; you know nothing could have persuaded me to write this but the pure desire of praising your mercy, so that after my death many who read it may be moved with compassion by the great goodness of your mercy. They will consider that, in your solicitude for humanity's salvation, your love has never descended so low as it has done in permitting so many and such great gifts to be held so cheap and to be treated as I have treated them, alas, spoiling everything you gave me.

But I give you thanks as best I can, Lord God, who have created and re-created me, for your merciful clemency, and for this assurance you have given me in your inexhaustible love, flowing down from on high.

(*Book* II:23)

Angela of Foligno

ca.1248–1309

Introduction

Angela was born about eight years before Gertrude and died seven years after her. However, I have placed Gertrude first because she is typical of the older, more traditional monastic spirituality that was far removed from that of the ecstatic woman of Foligno who became known to her followers as "Mother Angela." Also, Angela's spiritual journey began after Gertrude's, and was linked to the new movements then sweeping Christendom in the wake of the Crusades, giving rise to new attitudes toward women in Church and society.

Angela represents those whose spiritual development was intertwined with the recently founded mendicant Orders, especially the Franciscans. The mendicants (termed friars or "brothers") were ready to bring the gospel to the common people where they were. They were to be found in cities and classrooms, leper houses and hospitals. They preached in market squares as well as in churches. They wanted to offer the human Christ, present in crib, cross and eucharist, to those on the margins of society, those lost in the move to the great cities, uprooted from the familiar agrarian rhythm of seasons and feasts which had tied them to the soil and a settled way of life.

As their popularity increased, the mendicants (Franciscans, Dominicans, Augustinians and Carmelites) found ways to incorporate the laity into their spiritual interpretation of the apostolic life by introducing the concept of a third order (the first and second orders being the professed friars and their feminine counterpart of enclosed nuns). Third order members, or tertiaries, were men and women enabled to share the spirituality of an Order while remaining in the lay state. This concept was instrumental in bringing an intense spiritual life out of the cloister and into the homes of ordinary people.

In 1285, about five years after Gertrude's conversion experience, and when Angela herself was thirty-seven, this married woman, caught up in the ferment left in the wake of Francis of Assisi, the "Christ of Umbria," embarked on a path that was gradually to lead her to the heights of union with God. In the course of that ascent she describes thirty steps by which she scaled the heights of transformation into Christ, and which took place consecutively over a long period of time. During the early stages of her spiritual journey Angela's mother, husband, and sons all died, leaving her free to follow the path of total poverty and detachment to which she felt called so strongly that she could brook no obstacle standing in her way.

From what we can glean from her writings Angela came from a wealthy family of Foligno, a town some ten miles south of Assisi. Her early life was spent in the usual pleasures and pastimes of a well-to-do wife and mother. She enjoyed dressing in fine clothes and jewelry; she reveled in dancing and society gossip, all of which she later saw as direct impediments to loving God with her whole heart. She also seems to have been tormented by an unconfessed serious sin (presumably of a sexual nature) and finally confessing it took enormous courage on her part. She saw Saint Francis, her spiritual friend and father, as having had a direct influence on arranging for her to meet and confide in a friar, Brother Arnaldo, a distant relative who would later make a record of Angela's experiences for posterity.

In her spiritual ascent from worldly woman to woman of God, Angela is amazingly original and passionate. A passionate lover in the flesh she became one likewise in the spirit. Arnaldo, recording her experiences as she spoke in her native Umbrian dialect and translating them into Latin, said that he could not keep up with the torrent of ecstatic words that flowed from her. Inevitably he was compelled to compress her utterances into forms that satisfied neither Angela nor himself. As a woman Angela saw love as the motivating force of her life; but she was aware of its perils and its need for regulation and discipline if it was to bear fruit in good works and transcendent devotion.

The Franciscan movement made it possible for Angela to find a place for herself in the Order as a laywoman, rather like the beguines of

Northern Europe, instead of within the more formal monastic structures of the Benedictines or even the Poor Clares. In her penance, which she saw as both proof and enabler of love, Angela was carried along by an ardent and all consuming devotion to Christ crucified, wishing only for complete transformation into him. Her way of speaking has nothing of the measured tones of Gertrude in her monastery, with its liturgical rhythm and structured timetable giving pattern and meaning to daily work and prayer. Angela strips herself naked before Christ crucified as Francis had done; she is transported in spirit to the place of Calvary, clings to the cross, sings of poverty with ardent abandon. At the beginning of her mystical experience, when she is on pilgrimage to Assisi and feels the Holy Spirit to be within her, speaking to her in tones of tenderness, assuring her of being loved and chosen, she cannot contain the bliss she feels, and ends by screaming and shouting to release some of the emotion that overwhelms her senses as well as her spirit.

When Angela found herself freed from all family ties and securely embarked on the path of penance as a Franciscan tertiary she withdrew to a small dwelling with one woman companion, Masazuola. Masazuola, who was also renowned for her holiness of life, took the part of servant and chaperone, sharing in Angela's charitable works and making sure that she had her daily needs provided for. Angela then formally renounced all worldly pleasures and possessions and spent her time in prayer and service to the needy, meanwhile instructing a growing band of disciples—friars and lay men and women—in the ways of the spirit, so much so that she was revered as one who kept the true spirit of Saint Francis alive at a time when he was no longer present to his devotees in the flesh.

Poverty for Angela had a specific attraction. She wanted to be poor inwardly and outwardly. She wanted nothing but God to be her Lover and her reward. For her, as for other early Franciscans, Christ the poor man *par excellence* was present in the sick, the destitute, and the outcasts, such as lepers. One of Angela's most celebrated passages is where she and her companion visit the lepers and she forces herself to drink the water in which she has cleansed their sores. Instead of finding it repulsive, a particle of leprous scab lodged in her throat proves to be as sweet as receiving the host in Holy Communion.

In prayer Angela focuses very particularly on the suffering God-man, Jesus Christ, whom she learns of in the "Book of Life," i.e., the earthly life of Jesus as proclaimed and lived within the Franciscan gospel tradition, and whose founder received the stigmata, or impression of the wounds of Christ in his own flesh. Angela's vision, in which she seemed to be embraced by the Crucified, is a familiar Franciscan image, and the cross plays an increasingly important part in Angela's spiritual journey as a focus for her devotion and an impetus to penance and poverty. However, at the summit of her spiritual ascent it is a vision of the Virgin on the feast of the Presentation of Christ in the temple that confirms her in union with God. She knows herself fully offered and fully accepted, after a period of terrifying darkness, during which she felt herself doomed to eternal punishment and in the grip of the devil.

Angela's experiences were recorded by her scribe and confessor, the faithful friar Arnaldo, in the book of her *Memorial*. Arnaldo chronicles the stages of Angela's ascent through the steps toward union with God, sometimes writing in the third person, sometimes using the direct speech of Angela in the first person. The second part of Angela's book, contained in the *Instructions*, seems to have been compiled from various sources after the completion of the *Memorial*. Angela's life still had thirteen more years to run after the *Memorial* was finished, and she continued to teach and speak with her disciples, as well as to dictate letters which were collected for posterity. The *Instructions* are therefore of a more didactic nature, where Angela imparts teaching on prayer and on the virtues that should characterize a true follower of Christ. She has a most tender love for those she calls "her sons," and she wants them to partake of her spiritual insights and live for God without reserve. This marks the generative stage of Angela's life when she realizes that she has a mission to others, in which we can well include ourselves.

In choosing texts from Angela's *Complete Works* I have made use of the volume on Angela in the Classics of Western Spirituality series published by Paulist Press in 1993 and translated by Paul Lachance, O.F.M. I begin with something of Angela's chronological ascent in the early stages, then go on to some more descriptive visions, interspersed with her teaching. Angela's definition of prayer as "that in which God is found" is one of the most incisive in spiritual literature, and her three stages of prayer are practical and illuminating. Especially noteworthy is the fact that Angela says that she finds prayer of the body a necessity that is not left behind in the higher stages of contemplation. We can all practice this basic bodily prayer. Whether God wants to lead us further is neither our business nor within our conscious control. It is for us to do what we can; the rest is up to God. Listening to this ecstatic woman of Foligno is an education in passionate love that has few equals. Angela surrendered herself completely to the divine Lover, and he surpassed her expectations a thousand times over.

Angela's Spiritual Journey

First steps on way of penance and perfection

The first step is the awareness of one's sinfulness, in which the soul greatly fears being damned to hell. In it the soul weeps bitterly.

The second step is the confession of sins. In this step the soul still feels only shame and bitterness. It does not feel love, only grief. . . .

The third step is the penance the soul performs in satisfaction to God for its sins, and it is still grief-stricken.

The fourth step is the growing awareness of divine mercy. . . .

The fifth step is the knowledge of self. . . .

You need to be aware also that each of these steps takes time. It is indeed very pitiful and truly heartbreaking that the soul is so sluggish and moves so painfully and ponderously toward God. It takes such tiny steps at a time. As for myself, I lingered and wept at each step. My only consolation was in being able to weep, but it was a bitter consolation.

The sixth step consists of a certain illumination through which my soul was graced with a deeper awareness of all my sins. . . . And then, I was given to pray with a great fire of love. . . .

In the seventh step I was given the grace of beginning to look at the cross on which I saw Christ had died for us. What I saw was still without savor, but it did cause me much grief.

In the eighth step, while looking at the cross, I was given an even greater perception of the way the Son of God had died for our sins. . . . This perception of the meaning of the cross set me so afire that . . . I stripped myself of all my clothing and offered my whole self to him.

In the ninth step, it was given to me to seek the way of the cross, that I too might stand at the foot of the cross where all sinners find refuge. . . . This would entail forgiving all who had offended me, stripping myself of everything worldly, of all attachments to men and women, of my friends and relatives, and everyone else, and likewise of my possessions and even my very self. Then I would be free . . . to give my heart to Christ from whom I had received so many graces, and to walk along the thorny path, that is, the path of tribulation. . . .

In the tenth step, while I was asking God what I could do to please him more, in his mercy he appeared to me many times, both while I was asleep and awake, crucified on the cross. He told me that I should look at his wounds. . . . And he said: "I have endured all these things for you."

(*Memorial* I)

The fire of love in Angela's soul

(Christ speaks to his "faithful one") "Here then is the sign which I deposit in the depths of your soul . . . I deposit in you a love of me so great that your soul will be continually burning for me. So ardent will be this love that if anyone should speak to you offensively you will take it as a grace and cry out that you are unworthy of such a grace. Know that I myself suffered from such offences and my love for you was so great that I bore it all patiently. Through such experiences then, you will know that I am with you. And if perchance there is no one to speak offensively to you, you will nonetheless have a great desire to be so offended. When this happens it is a sure sign of the grace of God, for I myself bore such offences with great humility and patience."

(*Memorial* IV)

Angela's bed

I am in the God-man almost continually. It began in this continual fashion on a certain occasion when I was given the assurance that there was no intermediary between God and myself. Since that time there has not been a day or night in which I did not experience this joy of the humanity of Christ.

At this moment my desire is to sing and praise:

> I praise you God my beloved;
> I have made your cross my bed.
> For a pillow or cushion
> I have found poverty,
> and for other parts of the bed,
> suffering and contempt to rest on.

(Memorial IX)

Angela's pilgrimage and the beginning of her mystical experiences

She started by saying that during her trip to Assisi (about which I was questioning her), she was in a state of prayer all along the way. And among other things, she had asked blessed Francis to ask God on her behalf that she might feel Christ's presence; and likewise obtain from him the grace of observing well the rule of blessed Francis which she had recently promised; and above all for this: that he would make her become, and remain to the end, truly poor.

She so desired to attain a state of perfect poverty that for this purpose she had gone to Rome to ask the blessed Peter to obtain this for her from Christ. . . .

It was then, when she was on her way to the church of Saint Francis that she asked him—that is, blessed Francis—that he obtain for her the aforesaid graces from the Lord Jesus Christ. She related many other things which she had asked for in the prayer she was making on her way to Assisi. And when she reached the crossroads that lies between Spello and Assisi, at the junction of three roads, on a narrow path that leads to Assisi, it was said to her: "You prayed to my servant Francis but I did not want to send you any other messenger than myself. I am the Holy Spirit who comes to you to give you a consolation which you have never tasted before. I will accompany you and be within you until you reach Saint Francis's church; and no one will notice it. I wish to speak with you on the path and there will be no end to my speaking. You will not be able to do otherwise than listen because I have bound you fast. And I will not leave you until the second time you enter the church of Saint Francis. Then this particular consolation will leave you, but I will never leave you if you love me."

Then he began to say: "My daughter, my dear and sweet daughter, my delight, my temple, my beloved daughter, love me, because you are very much loved by me; much more then you could love me." Very often he also said: "My daughter and my sweet spouse." And he further added: "I love you so much more than any other woman in the valley of Spoleto. I have found a place to rest in you; now in turn place yourself and find your rest in me. You prayed to my servant Francis and because my servant Francis loved me very much, I, therefore, did much for him. And if there were any other person who loved me still more, I would do even more for him. And I will do for you what I did for my servant Francis, and more if you love me."

These words stirred up great doubts in me and my soul said to him: "If indeed you were the Holy Spirit, you would not say such things to me for it is not fitting. I am frail and these words could be a source of pride and vanity for me." To this he responded: "Think for a moment and see for yourself if all these words can become a source of pride and vanity for you; try even to get away from these words if you can." I then did what I could to produce vanity in myself in order to test whether what he said was true, and if he was indeed the Holy Spirit. I even also began to look around me in an effort to get away from these words. But wherever I looked I could hear him saying: "This is my creature." At that I felt a sweetness, an ineffable divine sweetness. . . .

There is no way that I could possibly render an account of how great was the joy and sweetness I was feeling, especially when I heard God tell me: "I am the Holy Spirit who enters into your deepest self."

. . . During my return by way of this Saint Francis road, he told me among other things: "I give you this sign that I am the one who is speaking and who has spoken to you. You will experience the cross and the love of God within you. This sign will be with you for eternity." And immediately I felt that cross and that love in the depths of my soul, and even the bodily repercussions of the presence of the cross; and feeling all this, my soul melted into the love of God.

(*Memorial* III)

Christ in the leper

On Maundy Thursday I suggested to my companion that we go out to find Christ: "Let's go," I told her, "to the hospital and perhaps we will be able to find Christ there among the poor, the suffering, and the afflicted," We brought with us all the head veils that we could carry, for we had nothing else. We told Giliola, the servant at the hospital, to sell them and from the sale to buy some food for those in the hospital to eat. And, although initially she strongly resisted our request, and said we were trying to shame her, nonetheless, because of our repeated insistence, she went ahead and sold our small head veils and from the sale bought some fish. We had also brought with us all the bread which had been given to us to live on.

And after we had distributed all that we had, we washed the feet of the women and the hands of the men, and especially those of one of the lepers which were festering and in an advanced stage of decomposition. Then we drank the very water with which we had washed him. And the drink was so sweet that, all the way home, we tasted its sweetness and it was as if we had received Holy Communion. As a small scale of the leper's sores was stuck in my throat, I tried to swallow it. My conscience would not let me spit it out, just as if I had received Holy Communion.

(*Memorial* V)

Vision of Christ in the host

On another occasion she said she had seen the Christ Child in the host. He appeared to her as someone tall and very lordly, as one holding dominion. He also seemed to hold something in his hand as a sign of his dominion, and he sat on a throne. But I cannot say what he was holding in his hands. I saw this with my bodily eyes, as I did everything I ever saw of the host. When this vision occurred I did not kneel down like the others and I cannot recall whether I ran right up to the altar or whether I was unable to move because I was in such a delightful contemplative state. I know that I was also very upset because the priest put down the host on the altar too quickly. Christ was so beautiful and so magnificently adorned. He looked like a child of twelve. This vision was a source of such joy for me that I do not believe I shall ever lose the joy of it. I was also so sure of it that I do not doubt a single detail of it. Hence it is not necessary to write it. I was even so delighted by that vision that I did not ask him to help me nor did I have anything good or bad to say. I simply delighted in seeing that inestimable beauty.

(*Memorial* III)

The world is pregnant with God

Immediately the eyes of my soul were opened, and in a vision I beheld the fullness of God in which I beheld and comprehended the whole of creation, that is, what is on this side and what is beyond the sea, the abyss, the sea itself, and everything else. And in everything that I saw, I could perceive nothing except the presence and power of God, and in a manner totally indescribable. And my soul in an excess of wonder cried out: "This world is pregnant with God!" Wherefore I understood how small is the whole of creation—that is, what is on this side and what is beyond the sea, the abyss, the sea itself, and everything else—but the power of God fills it to overflowing. He then said to me: "I have manifested to you something of my power." And from this I comprehended that henceforth I would be able to better understand other things.

(Memorial VI)

The furrow

I saw in myself two sides and it was as if these had been separated by a furrow. On one side I saw fullness of love and every good which was from God and not from me. On the other side I saw myself as arid and saw that nothing good originated in me. By this I discovered that it was not I who loved—even though I saw myself as total love—but that which loved in me came from God alone. Afterward God's love and mine converged, which brought about an even greater and more burning love than before. As a result, my desire was to hasten toward that love.

(Memorial VII)

God discloses himself to the soul

Immediately upon presenting himself to the soul, God likewise discloses himself and expands the soul and gives it gifts and consolations which the soul never before experienced. . . . In this state, the soul is drawn out of all darkness and granted a greater awareness of God than I would have thought possible. This awareness is of such clarity, certitude, and abysmal profundity that there is no heart in the world that can ever in any way understand it or even conceive it. Even my own heart cannot think about it by itself, or ever return to it to understand or even conceive anything about it. This state only occurs when God, as a gift, elevates the soul to himself, for no heart by itself can in any way expand itself to attain it. Therefore there is absolutely nothing that can be said about this experience, for no words can be found or invented to express or explain it; no expansion of thought or mind can possibly reach to those things, they are so far beyond everything—for there is nothing which can explain God. I repeat there is absolutely nothing which can explain God. Christ's faithful one affirmed with utmost certitude and wanted it understood that there is absolutely nothing which can explain God.

(*Memorial* IX)

The depths of the soul where God abides

Even if at times I can still experience outwardly some little sadness and joy, nonetheless there is in my soul a chamber in which no joy, sadness, or enjoyment from any virtue, or delight over anything that can be named, enters. This is where the All Good, which is not any particular good resides, and it is so much the All Good that there is no other good. Although I blaspheme by speaking about it—and I speak about it so badly because I cannot find words to express it—I nonetheless affirm that in this manifestation of God I discover the complete truth. In it I understand and possess the complete truth that is in heaven and in hell, in the entire world, in every place, in all things, in every enjoyment in heaven and in every creature. And I see all this so truly and certainly that no one could convince me otherwise. Even if the whole world were to tell me otherwise, I would laugh it to scorn. Furthermore, I saw the One who is and how he is the being of all creatures. I also saw how he made me capable of understanding those realities I have just spoken about better than when I saw them in that darkness which used to delight me so. Moreover, in that state I see myself as alone with God, totally cleansed, totally sanctified, totally true, totally upright, totally certain, totally celestial in him. And when I am in that state I do not remember anything else.

On one occasion, while I was in that state, God told me: "Daughter of divine wisdom, temple of the beloved, beloved of the beloved, daughter of peace, in you rests the entire Trinity; indeed, the complete truth rests in you, so that you hold me and I hold you." One of the effects of that state in my soul is to greatly increase my delight and understanding of how God comes in the sacrament of the altar accompanied by his host.

When I leave that supreme state in which I do not remember anything else, I come back and see myself in those good things I have just spoken about, but at the same time I see myself completely full of sin and obedient to it, devious, impure, totally false and erroneous, and yet I am in a state of quiet. For what remains with me is a continual divine unction, the highest of all and superior to any I have ever experienced in my life.

(*Memorial* IX)

Angela's soul presented to God

During the period when that unspeakable manifestation of God was occurring in my soul, one day, on the feast of Saint Mary of Candlemas, while blessed candles were being distributed for the celebration of the presentation of the Son of God in the temple, and at that very moment when this unspeakable manifestation of God was taking place, my soul experienced its own presentation. And it saw itself so noble and elevated that, henceforth, I cannot conceive or even imagine that my soul, or even the souls in paradise, could be or are endowed with such nobility. My soul then could not comprehend itself. If the soul, which is created, finite, and circumscribed, cannot comprehend itself, will it not be far less able to comprehend God, the creator, who is immense and infinite? My soul, then, immediately presented itself before God with the utmost assurance and without any fear. This presentation was accompanied with greater delight than I have ever experienced, with a new and most excellent joy, and with new miracles, so much so that I cannot imagine that my soul ever experienced anything so miraculous, so clear, and so new. Such was this encounter with God. In this encounter I simultaneously perceived and experienced both that previous unspeakable manifestation of God to my soul, and this new manifestation of my soul and its presentation to God. In this I found new delights different from all previous delights, and I was told most high words which I do not want to be written.

After this, when I returned to myself, I discovered that I was glad to suffer every injury and pain for God, and that nothing anyone could say or do henceforth could separate me from him. And I cried out: "Lord what can henceforth separate me from you?" In response, I was told that there was nothing that could separate me from God. Furthermore I delighted in the thought of my death. One cannot imagine the delight that is mine when I think of the day of my death.

(*Memorial* IX)

The perfection of love

This is the sign of those whose friendship with the supreme Being is divine and are true followers of his only Son: those who are in this state always have the eyes of the spirit turned toward him so that they love him, follow him, and transform themselves completely and totally according to the will of the Beloved, that is, the supreme Being.

(*Instructions* II)

In the Cross Is Salvation

The crucified Christ

Once when I was meditating on the great suffering which Christ endured on the cross, I was considering the nails, which, I had heard it said, had driven a little bit of the flesh of his hands and feet into the wood. And I desired to see at least that small amount of Christ's flesh which the nails had driven into the wood. And then such was my sorrow over the pain that Christ had endured that I could no longer stand on my feet. I bent over and sat down; I stretched out my arms on the ground and inclined my head on them. Then Christ showed me his throat and his arms.

And then my former sorrow was transformed into a joy so intense that I can say nothing about it. This was a new joy, different from the others. I was so totally absorbed by this vision that I was not able to see, hear, or feel anything else. My soul saw this vision so clearly that I have no doubts about it, nor will I ever question it. I was so certain of the joy which remained in my soul that henceforth I do not believe I will ever lose this sign of God's presence. Such also was the beauty of Christ's throat and neck that I concluded that it must be divine. Through this beauty I concluded I was seeing Christ's divinity, and that I was standing in the presence of God; but of that moment that is all I remember seeing. I do not know how to compare the clarity and brightness of that vision with anything or any color in the world except, perhaps, the clarity and brightness of Christ's body, which I sometimes see at the elevation of the host.

(*Memorial* III)

Love of the cross

Grieve and lament, O soul, which must pass by the cross on which Christ died. What you must do is to place yourself before it to find your rest, for the cross is your salvation and your bed. You must find delight in it because therein is indeed your salvation. It is amazing how anyone can pass by the cross quickly and without stopping. If the soul fixed its attention on the cross it would always find fresh blood flowing from it. From this example I understood who are the legitimate sons of God.

Afterward, whenever I passed near a painting of the cross or the passion, it seemed to me that the representation was nothing in comparison with the extraordinary sufferings which really took place and which had been shown to me and impressed in my heart. This is why I no longer want to look at these paintings, because they seemed to me to signify almost nothing in comparison with what really happened.

(Memorial V)

Angela is embraced by the Crucified

Once I was at Vespers and was gazing at the cross. And while I was thus gazing at the cross with the eyes of the body, suddenly my soul was set ablaze with love; and every member of my body felt the greatest joy. I saw and felt that Christ was within me, embracing my soul with the very arm with which he was crucified. This took place right at the moment when I was gazing at the cross or shortly afterward. The joy that I experienced to be with him in this way and the sense of security that he gave me were far greater than I had ever been accustomed to.

Henceforth my soul remained in a state of joy in which it understood what this man, namely Christ, is like in heaven, that is to say, how we will see that through him our flesh is made one with God. This was a source of delight for my soul beyond words or description, and it was a joy that was abiding. . . .

My delight at the present is to see that hand which he shows me with the mark of the nails on it, and to hear him say: "Behold what I have suffered for you and for others." The joy which seizes my soul in this moment can in no way be spoken of. And in no way whatever can I be sad concerning the passion; on the contrary, my joy is in seeing this man, and to come to him. All my joy is now in this suffering God-man.

At times it seems to my soul that it enters into Christ's side, and this is a source of great joy and delight; it is indeed such a joyful experience to move into Christ's side that in no way can I express it or put words to it.

(*Memorial* VI)

The agony of the Mother of God

Another time, I was once standing in prayer and meditating sorrowfully on the passion of the Son of God incarnate. Then through God's will, the passion was shown to me, that is, he himself granted me to see more of his passion than I have ever been told, and he saw that I perceived more of his passion than I have ever heard spoken of. For Christ had foreseen all the hearts impiously hardened against him, everyone contriving to destroy his name, and how they constantly kept in mind their purpose to destroy him. He had also foreseen all the subtle cunning they employed against him, the Son of God; their manifold designs and plans, and the extent of their rage against him; all their preparations and everything they thought about how they could even more cruelly afflict him—for the cruel sufferings of his passion were indeed acute and manifold. . . .

Then my soul cried out loudly: "O holy Mary, mother of the afflicted one, tell me something of your son's pain which no one else but you can possibly recall. For you saw more of his passion than any other saint; and as I perceive it, you not only saw with your bodily eyes, but also pictured it with your imagination, and out of the continual ardent devotion that was yours toward the one you loved." At this point, my soul cried out in extreme pain: "Is there any saint who can tell me something of this passion which I have not yet heard spoken of or related, but which my soul has seen, which is so great that I find no words to express it?" My soul saw such suffering! . . .

My pain, then, exceeded by far any that I had ever experienced. That my body could not sustain me then should not be cause for wonder, for at that point I could feel no joy. I indeed lost my usual capacity for joy, and during this period it was impossible for me to recover it.

(*Memorial* VII)

Fix your eyes on the God-man

I beg you with all my being not to turn the eyes of your soul away from the suffering God-man. If you keep your eyes fixed on him, your entire soul will be set ablaze. But if you are not doing so, strive with all your being to fix your eyes on him and keep them there. Moreover, my son, I desire with all my heart that your soul be elevated to see this suffering God-man, for this pleases me very much. But if your soul is not thus elevated, go back to yourself, start from the beginning and review from head to foot all the ways in which the suffering God-man was afflicted and crucified. If you cannot regain and rediscover these ways in your heart, repeat them vocally, attentively and frequently; because what the lips say and repeat grants fervor and warmth to the heart.

(*Instructions* XVIII)

"My love for you has not been a hoax"

On Wednesday of Holy Week, I was meditating on the death of the Son of God incarnate, and trying to empty my soul of everything else so I could be more recollected in his passion and death.

I had only one care, only one desire, and that was to find the best way to empty my soul from everything else in order to have a more vivid memory of the passion and death of the Son of God.

Suddenly, while I was engrossed in this effort and desire, a divine word sounded in my soul: "My love for you has not been a hoax." These words struck me a mortal blow. For immediately the eyes of my soul were opened and I saw that what he said was most true. I saw his acts of love, everything that the Son of God had done, all that he had endured in life and death—this suffering God-man—because of his inexpressible and visceral love. Seeing in him all the deeds of true love, I understood the perfect truth of what he had said, that "his love for me had not been a hoax," but that he had loved me with a most perfect and visceral love. I saw, on the other hand, the exact opposite in myself, because my love for him had never been anything but playing games, never true. Being made aware of this was a mortal blow and caused such intolerable pain that I thought I would die.

Suddenly other words came to increase my sorrow. After he had said, "My love for you has not been a hoax"—and I had perceived that this was true on his part but quite the contrary on mine, and I had felt such pain that I thought I would die—he added: "I have not served you only in appearance" and then "I have not kept myself at a distance, but have always felt you close to me."

These word increased my mortal pain and suffering even more. My soul cried out: "O Master, that which you assure me is not in you, is totally in me. My love for you has never been anything but a hoax and a lie. Nor have I ever really wanted to come close to you and feel the sufferings which you have endured for me. Furthermore, I have never served you, except in appearance and not truly." I perceived all the signs and marks of the truest love in him; how he had given himself wholly and totally to me, in order to serve me; how he had come so close to me. He had become human in order to truly feel and carry my sufferings in himself. When, on the other hand, I perceived the exact opposite in me, I had such suffering and pain that I thought I would die. I felt my ribs dislocate in my chest under the weight of my pain, and it seemed as though my heart would burst.

(*Instructions* XXIII)

Imitation of the passion of Christ is easy

Christ's faithful one once told me that she had heard God tell her that it is easy for those for whom Christ died to die for him; it is easy for those for whom he suffered to suffer for him; it is easy for those for whom he was despised to be despised for him.

(*Instructions* XXIV)

About Poverty and Penance

True poverty

Divine wisdom teaches this truth about poverty: It makes a person first see their own defects, then discover their own poverty and how truly one is poor in being. Thus illumined by the gift of divine grace, one sees the goodness of God. Then all doubt concerning God is immediately taken away, and one loves God totally; and loving with this love one performs works in accordance with this love, and then all self-reliance is taken away. When somebody possesses this truth, not all the devils there are, nor all the things we could possibly say, could ever deceive them. For the soul receives therein the most clear and luminous teaching on everything about this life, and in such a way that as long as it possesses this truth, it can never be deceived. This is why I understand that poverty is the mother of all virtues and the teacher of divine wisdom.

(*Memorial* VII)

Poverty and suffering, the heritage of the Son and sons of God

For all his life the suffering God-man knew only one state: that of the cross. His life began on the cross, continued on the cross, and ended on the cross. He was always on the cross of poverty, continual pain, contempt, true obedience, and other harsh deeds of penance. Since the heritage of the father should be handed down to his sons, God the Father handed the heritage of the cross and penance to his only Son. As a consequence, it is fitting that all the sons of God, the more they reach perfection, assume the heritage and adhere to its implications all their life. For the entire life of the suffering God-man was filled with the most bitter effects of the cross and penance. How long does penance last, and how much of it is there? As long as one lives. And as much as one can bear. This is the meaning of being transformed into the will of God. But when the soul is truly transformed into the will of God, or within God, and is in that state of perfect union and enjoys the full vision of him, it seeks nothing more. When, however, it is not in this state it strains to transform itself into the will of the Beloved until it recovers this state. And the suffering God-man demonstrates his will by the works of the cross and of penance which are always with him.

The more perfect one is and the more one loves God, the more one tries to do what the suffering God-man does and avoid whatever is contrary to God's will. Does not someone who loves another perfectly try to conform to the other's ways and do those things that please the loved one more? . . .

Take a good look at our father, the blessed Francis. He was a mirror of holiness and every perfection, the model for all those who wish to live the spiritual life. When he was near the end of his life, even though his state of perfection was so excellent and his union with God so ineffable, nonetheless, he said: "Brothers, let us begin to do penance for until now we have made little progress."

(*Instructions* II)

The necessity of penance

The sign that true love is at work is this: The soul takes up its cross, that is, penance as long as one lives, penance as great and harsh as possible.

When love is done with the works of the cross and penance in me, that is, after it has pushed these to their final limits, as long as I live and as harsh as possible, then I will become aware that in truth I am an unprofitable servant. And if I wish to ask God for

something, I will do it in the name of the penance he did in me
and for me. This is the sign of the spirit of truth: to realize that
God's being is total love and to acknowledge oneself as total hate.

Once the soul has this knowledge, it follows that it must
commit itself to bodily penance. . . . We should not be surprised
if the soul is weighed down by penance because the true Teacher
came to do penance for us: Throughout his entire life he experienced the bitterness of penance and the cross for us. Those who
are elevated to the vision of the Uncreated and the being of God
will find rest in the cross and in virtuous deeds wherever they
occur. Their love will be constantly renewed, and they will be set
ablaze to act more courageously. Those who are not in the truth
will make idols for themselves out of the virtuous deeds they
perform. And their first idol will be the divine light given to
them.

(*Instructions* II)

Three examples of true poverty

We have an example of true poverty in Jesus Christ, God and
man. This God and man Jesus Christ raised us up and redeemed
us by poverty. His poverty was truly ineffable, for it concealed so
much of his total power and nobility. He let himself be blas-
phemed, vilified, verbally abused, seized, dragged, scourged and
crucified, and through it all he always behaved as one powerless
to help himself. His poverty is a model for our life; we should
follow his example. . . .

We have another example of true poverty in the glorious
Virgin Mary, the most holy mother of God. She taught us this
poverty clearly when, in response to the news of the great
mystery of the incarnation, she declared herself to be of our
corrupted flesh and referred to herself as most lowly. . . .

We have yet another example of true poverty in the good thief
who was crucified with the God and man Jesus Christ. He had
lived an evil life and done wicked deeds; but once he received the

divine light and truly saw the goodness of God, he immediately saw his own poverty, acknowledged it, and answered his companion who was insulting Christ: "You are under the same condemnation as this man. Is there no fear of God in you? We are receiving what we deserve, but he has done no wrong." And turning to Christ he said: "Remember me, Lord, when you come into your kingdom." At that moment he was saved.

For us sinners, I see no better satisfaction we can make to God for our sins than by fully acknowledging our poverty.

(*Instructions* III:3)

About Prayer

The necessity of prayer

No one can be saved without divine light. Divine light causes us to begin and to make progress, and it leads us to the summit of perfection. Therefore if you want to begin and to receive this divine light, pray. If you have begun to make progress and want this light to be intensified within you, pray. And if you have reached the summit of perfection and want to be superillumined so as to remain in that state, pray.

If you want faith, pray. If you want hope, pray. If you want charity, pray. If you want poverty, pray. If you want obedience, pray. If you want chastity, pray. If you want humility, pray. If you want meekness, pray. If you want fortitude, pray. If you want some virtue, pray.

And pray in this fashion, namely, always reading the Book of Life, that is, the life of the God-man Jesus Christ, whose life consisted of poverty, pain, contempt and true obedience.

(*Instructions* III:2)

Jesus Christ, the Book of Life

Those who possess the spirit of true prayer will have the Book of Life, that is, the life of Jesus Christ, God and man, set before them, and everything they could want they will find there. Thus they will be filled with its blessed teaching—which does not puff anyone up—and will find there every doctrine that they and others need. Hence if you wish to be superenlightened and taught, read this Book of Life. If you do not simply skim through it but rather let it penetrate you while reading it, you will be taught everything needed for yourself and for others, no matter what your state of life. Also, if you read it carefully and not casually, you will be so inflamed by divine fire that you will accept every tribulation as the greatest consolation. It will even make you see that you are most unworthy of these tribulations, and what is more, if success or human praise should come your way because of whatever quality God has placed in you, you will not become vain or put on airs because of it. By reading in the Book of Life, you will see and know that, in truth, the praise is not meant for you. Not boasting or feeling superior about anything but always remaining humble is one of the signs by which one can detect that one is in a state of divine grace.

(Instructions III:2)

The benefits of prayer

The more you pray the more you will be enlightened; and the more you are enlightened, the more deeply and exaltedly you will see the supreme Good and what this supreme Good consists of; the deeper and more perfect your vision, the more you will love; the more you love, the more you will delight in what you see; the more you find delight, the more you will understand and be made capable of understanding. Afterward, you will come to the fullness of light because you will understand that you cannot understand.

(Instructions III:2)

Jesus Christ—our example of prayer

The Son of God, Jesus Christ in his human nature, himself gave us the example of the wonders of prayer and the need to persevere in it. He taught us how to pray in many ways through word and deed. Through words, he advised us to pray when he told his disciples: "Watch and pray lest you enter into temptation." You will find in many other places in the gospel the many ways he taught us how to say this venerable prayer, and how he let us know, by recommending it again and again, how dear it was to him. Loving us from the bottom of his heart, he wanted to take away every pretext we could have for neglecting this blessed prayer. This is why he said it himself, so that drawn by his example we would love this prayer above all others. The evangelist, in fact, says that through the intensity with which he said this prayer, his sweat became like drops of blood falling to the ground. Put this mirror before your eyes and strive with all your might to reproduce something of this prayer, for it was for you that he prayed, and not for himself. He was also teaching us how to pray when he said: "Father, if it is possible remove this chalice from me. Yet thy will be done, not mine." Notice how Christ always preferred the divine will to his own. Follow his example. He also taught us how to pray when he said: "Father, into your hands I commend my spirit." What more can one say? Jesus' whole life was a prayer because he was in a continual state of manifestation of God and self. Did Christ then pray in vain? Why, then, do you neglect prayer, when without prayer nothing can be obtained? Christ Jesus, true God and true man, prayed for you and not for himself so that you could have an example of true prayer. If you wish to obtain something from him, you must necessarily pray, for without prayer you cannot obtain it.

(*Instructions* III:2)

The three schools of prayer

It is in prayer that one finds God. There are three schools of prayer, that is three types of prayer, without which one does not find God. These are bodily, mental and supernatural.

Bodily prayer takes place with the sound of words and bodily movements such as genuflections. I never abandon this type of prayer. For sometimes when I want to devote myself to mental prayer I am impeded by my laziness or sleepiness. So I turn to bodily prayer, which leads to mental prayer. It should be done with attention. For instance, when you say the Our Father you should weigh carefully what you are saying. Do not run through it, trying to complete a certain number like little ladies doing piece work.

Prayer is mental when meditating on God so occupies the soul that one thinks of nothing but God. If some other thoughts come to mind I no longer call such prayer mental. Such prayer curbs the tongue and renders one speechless. . . .

I call prayer supernatural when God, bestowing this gift upon the soul and filling it with his presence, so elevates the soul that it is stretched, as it were, beyond its natural capacities. In this type of prayer the soul understands more of God than would be naturally possible. It knows that it cannot understand, and what it knows it cannot explain, because all that it sees and feels is beyond its own nature.

In these three schools of prayer you come to know who you are and who God is. From the fact that you know, you love. Loving, you desire to possess what you love. And this is the sign of true love: that the one who loves is transformed, not partially but totally into the Beloved.

(*Instructions* XXVIII)

The vision of God

The perfect and highest form of love, one without defects, is the one in which the soul is drawn out of itself and led into the vision and being of God. For when the soul is so drawn out of itself and led into this vision, it perceives how every creature has its being from the one who is the supreme Being; how all things and all that exists come to be through the supreme Being; how God is indeed the only one who has being, and that nothing has being unless it comes from him. The soul, drawn out of itself and led into this vision, derives from it an ineffable wisdom, one that is deep and mature. In this vision the soul discovers that only what is best comes from the supreme Being and it cannot deny this, for it sees in truth that all things that are from him are excellently made; things are done badly when we have destroyed those things he has made. This vision of the supreme Being also stirs up in the soul a love corresponding and proportionate to its object, for it teaches us to love everything which receives existence from the supreme Being. . . . When the soul sees the supreme Being stoop down lovingly toward creatures, it does likewise. Thus the supreme Being makes me love those who love him.

(*Instructions* II)

Angela as Mother and Teacher

On becoming little

I desire that you have in your souls what leads from discord to unanimity, namely, becoming little. When you are little you do not consider yourself self-sufficient because of your knowledge or your natural abilities, but rather you are inclined always to acknowledge your defects and your miserable condition. . . . This is what I desire for you my dearest ones, that by following this way of littleness and poverty, disciplined zeal and compassion, your life may be, even when your tongue is silent, a clear mirror for those who wish to follow this way, and a sharp-edged sword against the enemies of truth. . . .

My dearest ones, my soul will be greatly put at ease if I hear from you that having become little has made of you one heart and soul, for without this unity, in truth, I do not see how you can please God.

(*Instructions* IX)

On not judging others

Seeing the spiritual and corporeal misfortunes of a neighbor, those who lead the spiritual life do not become puffed up by their own well-being and presume to judge or despise that person. For enlightened by the light of humility the soul sees itself perfectly, and seeing itself it becomes aware, and even knows, that it has fallen in the same plight as its neighbor; or, if it has not fallen, it knows and understands it was not able by itself alone to resist falling, but only by the help of God's grace. . . . For such a soul, judgment of one's neighbor is not a source of pride but rather a reason for being more humble.

(*Instructions* V)

The sign of true love

The first sign of true love is that the lover submits his will to that of the Beloved. And this most special and singular love works in three ways.

First, if the loved one is poor, one strives to become poor, and if scorned, to be scorned.

Second, it makes to abandon all other friendships which could be contrary to this love, and leaves behind father, mother, sister, brother, and all other affections contrary to the will of the Beloved.

Third, one can keep nothing hidden from the other. This third action, in my opinion, is the highest one and completes all the others. For in this mutual revelation of secrets, hearts are opened and bound more perfectly to one another.

(*Instructions* VI)

Bearing with others

Let us be indulgent toward those who offend us by word or deed, respond calmly, and not oppose them by taking note of the injury. It is with a calm exterior and a soul at rest that we must exercise indulgence to those who offend us, like a person who would willingly kiss the feet of those who offend him. To acquire this virtue one should look at Christ and see how he bore offenses with kindness. His example gives us strength not to hold a grudge. Finally, we should imitate Christ so as to remain straightforward in word and deed, without deception or duplicity.

(*Instructions* XXVIII)

The knowledge of God and self

Knowledge of God presupposes knowledge of self in the following manner: One must consider and see who is offended, and then consider and see who is the offender. From the insight derived from the second consideration, one is granted grace upon grace, vision upon vision, light upon light.

And from these one begins to attain knowledge of God. The more one knows, the more one loves; the more one loves, the more one desires; the more one desires, the more one grows in the capacity to act accordingly. How one acts is the sign and measure of love. And the test of pure, true, upright love is whether one loves and acts in accordance with the love and action of the loved one.

Christ the Beloved, always had, always loved, and always practiced poverty, suffering, and contempt. Therefore, like Christ, the one who loves him should always love, put into practice, and possess these three things.

(*Instructions* XXIX)

Knowing and loving God

Discovering that God is good, the soul loves him for his goodness. Loving him, it desires to possess him; desiring him, it gives all that it has or can have, even its own self, in order to possess him; and in possessing him, the soul experiences and tastes his sweetness. Possessing, experiencing, tasting God himself, the supreme and infinite sweetness, it enjoys him with the greatest delight.

Then, enamored with the sweetness of the Beloved, the soul desires to hold him; desiring to hold him, it embraces him; embracing him, it binds and weds itself to God, and finds God bound and wedded to itself in the sweetest form of love. Then the power of love transforms the lover into the Beloved and the Beloved into the lover. This means that, set ablaze by divine love, the soul is transformed by the power of love into God the Beloved whom it loves with such sweetness. . . .

For this transformation to happen, it is necessary that knowledge come first, and the love follows which transforms the lover into the Beloved. This is how the soul which knows God in truth and loves him with fervor is transformed into the Good it knows and loves with such fervor.

(*Instructions* XXXIV)

Humility of heart—basis of all the virtues

Behold, my blessed sons, and observe the model of your life, the suffering God and man, and learn from him all perfection. Observe his life, be attentive to his teachings, and with all your affections run after him, so that led by him you may successfully attain the cross. He gave himself as an example, and he exhorts us to look at him with the eyes of the spirit as he says: "Learn from me, for I am meek and humble of heart and you shall find rest for your souls."

My sons, be attentive, look with your most profound gaze into the depths of this doctrine, the sublimity of this teaching. Note its basis and its roots. Christ did not say: "Learn from me to fast," although as an example to us and for our salvation he fasted forty days and forty nights. He did not say: "Learn from me to despise the world and live in poverty," although he lived in great poverty and wished his disciples to live in the same way. He did not say: "Learn from me to perform miracles," although he himself performed miracles by his own power and wished his disciples to do so in his name. But he said simply: "Learn from me because I am meek and humble of heart."

The truth of the matter is that he set forth humility of heart and meekness as the foundation and firmest basis of all the other virtues. For neither abstinence, severe fasting, outward poverty, shabby clothing, outward show of good works, the performance of miracles—none of these amount to anything without humility of heart. . . .

O my sons, where can a creature find rest and peace if not in him who is sovereign rest and peace, the sovereign source of peace and tranquillity for your souls? But no soul will be able to attain him if it is not grounded in humility. For without humility of heart all the other virtues by which one runs toward God seem—and are—absolutely worthless.

(*Instructions* V)

A remedy against temptation

There is another special remedy for all temptations. It consists in vividly calling to mind the virginity and uprightness which the mother of God possessed to a most singular degree. Keep in mind too how perfectly she loved these virtues, and how she loves to see them brought to perfection in all the sons of God. And we should look at how these virtues were loved by the God-man himself. The sight of this does two things: It chases away all temptations from us, and it teaches us to be totally circumcised inside and out. Therefore, my sons, may the memory of these virtues of the mother of God be always in your soul.

(*Instructions* VII)

Angela's spiritual legacy

Then I was told of all my spiritual sons in general: "These and all the others will be sources of joy for you." I had prayed that they would all be purified and be sources of joy for me. God himself purified them all and he said: "To your sons present and absent I will bestow the Holy Spirit who will set them ablaze and, through love, will transform them completely into my passion. This transformation, however, will vary greatly from one to another. The more they keep in mind my passion, the more they will have of my love; and the more of such love they have, the more they will be united to me." He added other things about these different degrees of transformation, but I no longer remember them. All this delighted me very much.

Then my soul was suddenly elevated and I saw the majesty of God in an utterly unspeakable way, more than I had ever seen him. I saw him embracing all my sons. He held some at his side, others close to his breast or face, and still others he embraced totally. He did so according to the degree of their transformation into the passion of Christ and his love. All of them, the first, the second, and the third, rejoiced to be in God's presence, but those who were totally embraced and faced God directly rejoiced indescribably more than the others. My own joy over this was also indescribable.

(*Instructions* XXVI)

Angela blesses her sons before her death

O my dear little sons, fathers and brothers, strive to love one another and to truly possess divine charity. Because of this charity and mutual love the soul deserves to inherit divine riches. I do not make any other testament except that I wish for you to have love for one another, and I leave you all I have inherited: the life of Christ, that is, poverty, suffering, and contempt.

She placed her hand on the head of each of us saying: May God bless you, as I do, my dear sons, you and all the others who are not here. As Christ has showed to me an eternal blessing and indicated its meaning to me, so do I bestow the blessing, with all my heart, on you, both present and absent. And may Christ himself bestow it on you with the hand which was nailed to the cross. Those who possess this inheritance, namely, the life of Christ, and become true sons of prayer, will without doubt later possess the heritage of eternal life.

(*Instructions* XXXVI)

Angela's prayer of praise

O incomprehensible charity! There is no greater charity than the one by which God became flesh in order that he might make me God! O heartfelt love poured out for me! When you assumed human form you gave of yourself in order to make me. You did not let go of anything in yourself in any way that would lessen you or your divinity, but the abyss of your conception makes me pour out these deep, heartfelt words: O incomprehensible one, made comprehensible! O uncreated one, made creature! O inconceivable one, made conceivable! O impalpable one, become palpable!

O Lord, make me worthy of seeing the depths of charity which you communicated to us in your most holy incarnation. O happy fault, which merited that we discover the most hidden depths of divine charity until then hidden from us! Oh, in truth, I cannot imagine anything greater to contemplate! O most high, make me able to understand this most high and ineffable charity.

(*Instructions* XXXV)

Birgitta of Sweden

1303–1373

Introduction

Like Angela, Birgitta was a married woman, but her spiritual development was along very different lines from that of her Umbrian counterpart. Although both had a deep devotion to the Poverello, Francis of Assisi, Birgitta was destined to play a part on the international scene in a way unusual for a woman. Her life and her *Revelations* form a seamless whole and cannot be separated. Like a true prophet she *lived* her message in her life, her words calling to account the powerful and the great, thus earning for her the title of "the Swedish Joan of Arc."

Birgitta was also to leave behind a permanent legacy in that she founded a religious Order, the Order of the Most Holy Savior, or "Brigittines" in common parlance. This would ensure that her memory and her teaching were conserved by a spiritual posterity who would revere her as "mother and foundress." Unfortunately, for most of Europe she was unknown until recently, since the Reformation in Sweden meant that she was eclipsed both as national figure and spiritual mentor.

Birgitta was born in 1302 or 1303 into the Swedish nobility, being a cousin of King Magnus. Her mother, when heavily pregnant with her, was rescued from a sinking ship, and the infant spent the first four years of her life mute. The child was one of those few who seem to be marked by God from an early age and never deviate from the path they see before them. Not for her the conversion experiences of an Angela of Foligno, or even a Saint Gertrude.

When barely eight years old Birgitta had her first vision, where she beheld our Lady holding a crown in her hand and saying: "Come, Birgitta, would you like to wear this crown?" And as she bent her head she distinctly felt the pressure of the crown being placed by our Lady's hands. Her next vision was of the crucified Jesus, who said to her: "See, my child, how they have wounded me." "My Lord, who has dared to treat you so?" asked the young Birgitta. To this Jesus replied "Those who reject and despise my love." This marked Birgitta henceforth with a deep devotion to the passion and wounds of the Savior, so much so that in the Order she founded the nuns wore on their heads the distinctive "Brigittine crown" with its five red points marked out on a white background in honor of Christ's sacred wounds.

At the age of thirteen Birgitta was married to Wulf, Prince of Nericia. It was a happy marriage and eight children were produced from their union. The third child, Katherine, would also be venerated as a saint, becoming the first abbess of Birgitta's monastery at Vadstena. Revelations continued all through Birgitta's life, causing her to be at odds with the high society among which she and her husband moved. When at court Birgitta felt compelled to remonstrate at the abuses and moral laxity she saw among the Swedish nobility, and eventually she and her husband left court and went on pilgrimage to the tomb of Saint Olav in Drontheim and then to Saint James in Compostella. On the way to Compostella the couple met the Cistercian Peter of Alvastra who would be Birgitta's confessor and spiritual companion for the remainder of her life.

When Wulf and Birgitta returned to Sweden after their pilgrimage Wulf entered the Cistercian monastery at Alvastra where he died three years later. Birgitta herself then resided at the same monastery for some time until a crisis of some sort called her forth to speak and to prophesy under a new title, that of "Bride of the Lord."

The first revelations that Birgitta received after this were to do with the Order she was destined to found at the castle of Vadstena. It was to be a mixed Order including both men and women. The nuns' main duty was to chant a special Office in honor of Our Lady, composed by the saint's chaplain, Peter of Skaning. The long lessons which made up a large part of this Office were known as *Sermo Angelicus* because they were said to have been dictated to Birgitta by an angel.

As the Church forbade any new Rules from being promulgated, Birgitta chose the Augustinian Rule, to which were added her own *Regula Salvatoris* as Constitutions. Unlike the English Gilbertines, who also lived in double monasteries under a ruling abbot, in Birgitta's monasteries the abbess was the main figure, symbolizing the Virgin Mary presiding over the gathering. Ideally each Brigittine monastery was to consist of sixty sisters, plus thirteen priests (the thirteen apostles including Paul), four deacons (for the four principal doctors of the Church), and eight lay brothers, with the men and women sharing the same Church but having separate living quarters and separate choirs, the nuns' choir being on a higher level. Altogether the number represented the thirteen apostles and seventy-two disciples with the Virgin Mary. While the nuns were strictly enclosed, the men were expected to preach, welcome pilgrims, and act as spiritual directors to the sisters. From the first, Birgitta's monasteries attracted a number of outstanding recruits. The Order counteracted the laxity prevalent in the older monastic communities, and was known for the high intellectual level that it exacted of its priests. This was shared with the women who formed the main part of the Order, and indeed are the only ones to survive to the present, the last monks dying out in the eighteenth century. The Brigittine Order was also the first monastic Order to have the Blessed Sacrament exposed on the altar for veneration outside of Mass.

It was while setting out to visit Vadstena with a view to founding her first monastery that Birgitta received the visions that comprise the fifth book of her *Revelations*. They consist in a series of questions and answers about matters of faith and morals, interspersed with "words" from the Virgin. All was compacted within the experience of an hour or so.

Once the building of the famous "blue church" at Vadstena was under way Birgitta turned her steps toward Rome to obtain permission for the new way of life she wanted to inaugurate. At that time the Pope was residing at Avignon and, like Catherine of Siena, Birgitta felt impelled to call for his return to the Holy City. While in Rome Birgitta was present for the Jubilee of 1350 and witnessed thousands coming on pilgrimage. From there she also undertook a number of reforming missions in the area, calling to account the rich and the powerful, becoming well known as a person to be reckoned with, her reputation for holiness going before her. While in Rome, Birgitta's daughter

Katherine joined her, sharing all her mother's aspirations now that she too was left a widow.

In 1367 the Pope returned to Rome, and Birgitta managed to obtain from him confirmation of her proposed Order and a blessing on Vadstena, where Katherine would later be installed as the first abbess. Meanwhile the Pope once again departed for Avignon where he was to die.

At seventy years of age Birgitta was commanded by our Lord to go on pilgrimage to Jerusalem, just as Angela had traveled to Rome and Assisi as part of her own spiritual journey. Birgitta set out with three of her children, Karl, Birgir and Katherine, traveling via Naples where she was received as a saint. In Palestine the party lodged with the Franciscans who had charge of all the Holy Places, and where Birgitta was left free to come and go as she pleased. Again she was blessed with visions and revelations regarding the life and passion of Christ and his mother, and these she faithfully recorded as part of her spiritual patrimony. Some have influenced subsequent iconography, especially her sight of the infant Christ laid on the ground after his birth while the Virgin kneels in adoration before him.

At length Birgitta turned homeward, stopping en route in Cyprus to proclaim further prophecies. It was in Rome that she was to meet her death, having been promised that she would be accepted mystically as nun, bride of Christ, and "mother" of the Vadstena community. In one of her last visions she, who had been dressed as a widow, was mystically clothed in the grey Brigittine habit, the distinctive crown of the five wounds adorning her black veil, and a ring of espousal to Christ on her finger.

After her death, Birgitta was brought back to Sweden where her body was buried at Vadstena and from whence her Order spread rapidly.

Although Birgitta was famous in her native Sweden during the Middle Ages, her memory suffered an eclipse at the Reformation, and apart from her Order's contemplative houses abroad her legacy was almost unknown. This began to change when a Swedish convert to Catholicism, Mother Elisabeth Hesselblad, recently beatified, founded a new branch of the Brigittine Order in Birgitta's former house in Rome. At the same time, interest in Birgitta as a national heroine was rekindled among the Protestant Swedes, a *Society of Saint Birgitta* was founded, and Mother Elisabeth's sisters were invited to her homeland to participate in celebrations marking the society's third anniversary. Vadstena is now once more a Brigittine monastery, and the two branches of the Order, old and new, have ensured a current interest in the saint as a woman with a significance for all time. Birgitta has been named by John Paul II as one of the principal patrons of Europe, together with Edith Stein who was killed in the Holocaust, and Catherine of Siena.

As the complete Revelations of Saint Birgitta are almost unobtainable even in her native Sweden, I have had to confine myself to what has been translated into English, that is: Book Five, *The Book of Questions*, so called because it is set out under the format of questions and answers about the Catholic faith and contains various direct "revelations" or "words" from the Virgin Mary; Book Seven, which recounts some of Birgitta's experiences in the Holy Land; and a selection from her prayers which exerted such a profound influence on Catholic devotion, especially the communities that followed her Rule. These are preceded by a few extracts from Birgitta's *Life*. Also included are some letters and prophecies which will give an idea of Birgitta's breadth of interest in and care for the Church. As a woman of substance and a member of the Swedish nobility she had a unique opportunity to speak out and be heard by those in the seats of power. Even so, it cannot have been an easy task. Birgitta is one of history's "strong women" who deserves to be better known.

The translation is from the Classics of Western Spirituality Series published by Paulist Press 1990, translated by Albert Ryle Kezel, edited and with a preface by Marguerite Tjader Harris.

Background to Birgitta's Prophetic Calling

The manner of Birgitta's revelations

In the year of our Lord 1345, the first divine revelations were made to Lady Birgitta not in sleep but while she was awake and at prayer, with her body remaining alive in its vigor . . . for she saw and heard spiritual things and felt them in spirit. Indeed, in the manner mentioned, she saw and heard corporeal images and similitudes; in fact, in her heart she felt something, as it were, alive, which moved more actively and more fervently in response to greater inflammations and infusion, but less when the infusions were less. Many times, indeed, the movement in her heart was so vehement that motion could be seen and felt even on the outside.

In the fourth year before her husband's passing, a saint of our land of Sweden, Botvid by name, appeared to her, as it were in an ecstasy of mind, and said: "I have, with other saints, merited for you God's grace—namely, to hear and to see and to feel spiritual things—and the Spirit of God will inflame your soul."

(*Life* 27-28)

Birgitta's mission foretold

When Lady Birgitta had come to [a certain] monastery and was residing there, this brother wondered in his heart and said: "Why does that lady settle here in a monastery of monks, introducing a new custom against our Rule?" Then this same brother was caught up in an ecstasy of mind and clearly heard a voice saying to him: "Do not wonder. This woman is a friend of God; and she has come in order that at the foot of this mountain she may gather flowers from which all people, even overseas and beyond the world's ends, shall receive medicine."

(*Life* 30)

Birgitta the Inspired One

Introducing the fifth book of the *Revelations*

Here begins the fifth book of Christ's heavenly revelations to blessed Birgitta of the kingdom of Sweden. It is deservedly entitled the *Book of Questions* because it proceeds by means of questions to which Christ the Lord gives wonderful solutions. It was revealed to that same lady in a wonderful way, as she and her confessors often testified in their own words. For it once happened that on a certain day, she was riding a horse and traveling to her castle in Vadstena in the company of many members of her household who were riding along with her. Then, as she was thus riding along the road, she began to raise her mind to God in prayer. And at once she was caught up in spirit and went, as it were, outside herself, alienated from the sense of her body and suspended in an ecstasy of mental contemplation. She saw then, in spirit, a ladder which was fixed in the earth and whose top touched the sky. And at its top, in the sky, she saw the Lord Jesus Christ seated on a wonderful throne like a judge judging. At his feet stood the Virgin Mary; and round about the throne there was an infinite army of angels and a teeming multitude of saints. And, in the middle of that same ladder, the aforesaid Lady Birgitta saw a certain religious, known to her and at that time still alive in the body—a man of great erudition in the science of theology but full of guile and diabolical malice. Because of his extremely impatient and restless gestures, this man looked more like a devil than a humble religious. And then the said lady saw the thoughts and all the internal affections of the heart of that religious and how he manifested them with inordinate and restless gestures, by means of questions to Christ the Judge seated on the throne—as follows below. And then the Lady Birgitta herself saw and heard in spirit how Christ the Judge, with most meek and dignified gestures, replied briefly to each question with great wisdom and how, at times, our Lady, the Virgin Mary, spoke some words to the same Lady Birgitta—as this book will show in greater detail below.

Moreover, after the lady had in her mind, in a single instant, the whole of this book by means of one and the same revelation, and while she was now approaching the aforementioned castle, the members of her household grasped the bridle of her horse and began to shake her and, as it were, to awaken her from that rapture. And when she had returned to herself, she was exceedingly grieved by the fact that she was now deprived of such divine sweetness.

This *Book of Questions* then remained fixed in her heart and her memory as effectively as if it had all been carved on a marble tablet. But she immediately wrote it out in her own language; and her confessor translated it into the literary tongue, just as he had been accustomed to translate the other books of revelations.

(*Revelations* V:Prologue)

First Interrogation

I saw a throne in the sky, and on it sat the Lord Jesus Christ as Judge. Before his feet sat the Virgin Mary; and around the throne there was an army of angels and an infinite number of saints. A religious, very learned in theology, stood on a high rung of a ladder that was fixed in the earth and whose summit touched the sky. His gestures were very impatient and restless, as if he were full of guile and malice. He questioned the Judge, saying:

First question. "O Judge, I ask you: You have given me a mouth. May I not say the things that please me?"

Second question. "You have given me eyes. May I not see with them those things which delight me?"

Third question. "You have given me ears. Why am I not to hear with them those things that please me?"

Fourth question. "You have given me hands. Why am I not to do with them what agrees with me?"

Fifth question. "You have given me feet. Why should I not walk with them as I desire?"

Christ's response to the first question. The Judge who sat on the throne and whose gestures were meek and very dignified, replied: "Friend, I gave you a mouth that you might speak rationally about things that are useful for your body and soul and about things that belong to my honor."

Response to the second question. "Second, I gave you eyes that you might see evils to be fled and healthful things to be kept."

Response to the third question. "Third, I gave you ears that you might hear those things that belong to truth and honesty."

Response to the fourth question. "Fourth, I gave you hands that you might do those things that are necessary for the body and not harmful to the soul."

Response to the fifth question. "Fifth, I gave you feet that you might draw back from love of the world and go to your soul's rest and love and to me, your Creator and Redeemer."

(*Revelations* V:1)

Words from the Virgin Mary

The Mother speaks: "Daughter, you must have five inward things and five outward. First outwardly: a mouth clean of all detraction, ears closed to idle talk, modest eyes, hands busy with good works, and withdrawal from the world's way of life. Item. Inwardly, you must have five things: namely, fervent love for God, a wise longing for him, the distribution of your temporal goods with a just and right intention and in a rational way, humble flight from the world, and a long-suffering and patient expectation of my promises."

(*Revelations* V:3; BVM 1)

The Mother speaks: "Which of the saints had the sweetness of the Spirit without first experiencing bitterness? Therefore, one who craves sweetness must not flee away from things that are bitter."

(*Revelations* V:5; BVM 2)

Christ praises his mother

The Son speaks: "I am a crowned king in my Godhead, without beginning and without end. A crown has neither beginning nor end, thus signifying my power which had no beginning and shall have no end. But I had still another crown in my keeping; and this crown is I myself, God. This crown was prepared for the one who had the greatest love for me; and you, my sweetest Mother, won it and drew it to yourself with your justice and your charity. For the angels and the other saints bear witness to the fact that in you there was a love for me more ardent than any other and a chastity more pure; and this pleased me more than all else. Truly, your head was like gleaming gold and your hair like the rays of the sun. For your most pure virginity—which in you is, as it were, the head of all your virtue—and your freedom from illicit impulses pleased me and shone in my sight with all humility. Therefore, you are deservedly called a crowned queen over all that is created: 'queen' because of your purity and 'crowned' because of your excellent dignity. Your brow was of an incomparable whiteness—signifying the modesty of your conscience, in which resides the fullness of human knowledge and in which the sweetness of divine wisdom shines upon all. Your eyes were so lucid in my Father's sight that in them he gazed upon himself; for, in your spiritual vision and in your soul's intellect, the Father saw all your will—that you wanted nothing but him and desired nothing which did not please him. Your ears were most pure and were open like the fairest windows when Gabriel made known my will to you and when I, God, became flesh in you. Your cheeks were of the finest color—namely, white and ruddy—for the fame of your praiseworthy deeds and the beauty of your character daily burning within you pleased me. At the beauty of your character God my Father truly rejoiced; and he never turned his eyes away from you. And, out of your love, all have obtained love. Your mouth was like a lamp—burning within and shining without—because the words and affections of your soul burned inwardly with divine understanding and shone outwardly in the praiseworthy control of your bodily motions and in the lovely harmony of your virtues."

(*Revelations* V: 9; BVM 4)

Birgitta drawn into the mansion of the Holy Spirit

The Son speaks to the bride: "You are she who was nurtured in a house of poverty and then came into the society of the great. In a house of poverty there are three things: namely, stained walls, harmful smoke, and pervasive soot. But you have been led into a house where there is beauty without stain, warmth without smoke, and sweetness that fills without cloying. The house of poverty is the world. Its walls are pride, oblivion of God, abundance of sin, and disregard of the future. These walls stain because they annihilate good works and hide God's face from mankind. The smoke is love of the world. It harms the eyes because it darkens the soul's understanding and causes the soul to worry about superfluous things. The soot is pleasure; for even if it delights for a time, it never satisfies or replenishes with eternal goodness. From these things therefore you were drawn away; and you were led into the mansion of the Holy Spirit. He is in me, and I am in him, and he encloses you in himself. He, indeed, is most pure and most beautiful and most steadfast; for he sustains all things. Therefore, conform yourself to the Inhabitant of the house by remaining pure, humble, and devout."

(*Revelations* V:13)

The enkindling of love in Birgitta's heart

The Son of God speaks: "By means of natural things, a healthful drink can be made—namely, of cold iron and hard stone, of a dry tree and a bitter herb. But how? Certainly, if steel were to fall upon a sulphurous mountain with force, then fire would go forth from the steel to ignite the mountain. Out of its warmth, an olive tree planted nearby—outwardly dry but inwardly full of unction—would begin to flow so greatly that the bitter herb, planted at the olive's foot would be sweetened by the downflow of oil; and thence a healthful drink could be made. This is what I have done for you in a spiritual way. For your heart was as cold toward my love as steel; and yet, in it there moved a modest spark of love for me, namely, when you thought me worthy of love and honor above all others. But that heart of yours then fell upon the sulphurous mountain when the glory and delight of the world turned against you and when your husband, whom you carnally loved beyond all others, was taken from you by death. In truth, mundane pleasure and delight are well compared to a sulphurous mountain; for they are accompanied by swollenness of the soul, the stench of concupiscence, and the burning of punishment. And when at your husband's death your soul was gravely shaken with disturbance, then the spark of my love—which lay, as it were, hidden and enclosed—began to go forth, for, after considering the vanity of the world, you abandoned your whole will to me and desired me above all things. And so, because of that spark of love, you relished the dry olive tree, i.e., the words of the gospels and the conversation of my Doctors, and abstinence so pleased you that all the things that previously seemed bitter began to be sweet for you. And when the oil began to flow and the words of my revelations came down upon you in spirit, then one stood upon the mountain and cried, saying: 'By this drink, thirst is quenched; the cold are warmed; the disturbed are gladdened; and the infirm convalesce.' It is I myself, God, who cry. My words—which you hear from me frequently in spiritual vision—like the good drink, satisfy those who thirst for true charity; second, they warm those who are cold; third, they gladden those who are disturbed; and fourth, they heal those who are weak in soul."

(*Revelations* V:15)

A figurative explanation of the graces received by pilgrims who visit the holy places of Jerusalem and Bethlehem

God the Father speaks: "There was a certain lord whose servant said to him: 'Behold, your fallow land has been cultivated and the roots have been pulled out; when is the wheat to be sown?' The lord said to him: 'Even though the roots seem to have been pulled out, nevertheless the hardened old trunks and stumps are still left. In spring, the rains and the winds are going to loosen them. Therefore, patiently wait the time for sowing.' To this the servant replied: 'What am I to do between the seasons of spring and harvest?' The lord said to him: 'I know five places. Everyone who goes to them shall have fivefold fruit if only he comes pure and empty of pride and warm in charity. In the first place there was a vessel, closed and not closed; a vessel small and not small; a vessel luminous and not luminous; a vessel empty and not empty; a vessel clean and not clean. In the second place, there was born a lion that was seen and not seen, that was heard and not heard, that was touched and not touched, that was recognized and was not known, that was held and not held. In the third place there was a lamb, shorn and not shorn; a lamb wounded and not wounded; a lamb calling and not calling; a lamb suffering and not suffering; a lamb dying and not dying. In the fourth place there was a serpent that lay and did not lay, moved and did not move, heard and did not hear, saw and did not see, felt and did not feel. In the fifth place there was an eagle that flew and did not fly, and that came to a place from which it had never withdrawn, that rested and did not rest, that was renewed and not renewed, that rejoiced and did not rejoice, that was honored and not honored.' "

The exposition and clarification of the things said above. The Father speaks: "That vessel of which I spoke to you was Mary, Joachim's daughter, the mother of Christ's human nature. She was indeed a vessel closed and not closed: closed to the devil but not to God. For just as a torrent—wishing to enter a vessel opposed to it and not being able—seeks other ways in and out, so the devil, like a torrent of vices, wished to approach Mary's heart by all his inventions; but he was never able to incline her soul toward even the slightest sin because it had been closed against his temptations. For the torrent of my Spirit had flowed into her heart and filled her with special grace. Second, Mary, the mother of my Son, was a vessel small and not small: small and modest in the contempt of her lowliness; great and not small in love for my Godhead. Third, Mary was a vessel empty and not empty: empty of all hedonism and sin; not empty but full of heavenly sweetness and goodness. Fourth, Mary was a vessel luminous and not luminous: luminous because every beautiful soul is created by me; but Mary's soul so grew toward the full perfection of light that my Son fixed himself in her soul, at whose beauty heaven and earth rejoiced. But this vessel was not luminous in the sight of mankind because she scorned the world's honors and wealth. Fifth, Mary was a vessel clean and not clean: truly clean because she was all beautiful and because there was not found in her even enough uncleanness in which to fix the point of a needle; not clean because she came forth from Adam's root and was born of sinners, although herself conceived without sin in order that, of her, my Son might be born without sin. Therefore, whoever comes to that place [Jerusalem], namely, where Mary was born and reared, will not only be cleansed but will also be a vessel to my honor.

"The second place is Bethlehem, where my Son was born like a lion. He was seen and held in his humanity; but in his Godhead he was invisible and unknown.

"The third place is Calvary, where my Son, like an innocent lamb, was wounded and died in his humanity; but in his Godhead he was impassible and immortal.

"The fourth place was the garden of my Son's sepulcher, in which his humanity was placed, and it lay like a contemptible serpent; but in his Godhead he was everywhere.

"The fifth place was Mount Olivet, from which my Son, like an eagle, flew up to heaven in his humanity; but in his Godhead he was always there. He was renewed and he rested in his humanity; but in his Godhead he was always at rest and always the same.

"Therefore, one who comes to these places pure and with a good and perfect will, will be able to see and taste how sweet and pleasant I, God, am. And when you come to these places I shall show you more."

(*Revelations* V:16)

Calling Others to Account

Birgitta as Christ's messenger

In that same hour, Christ spoke to his bride, Lady Birgitta, saying: "To these things that you have now seen and to the other things that I have endured, the world's princes are not attentive; nor do they consider the places in which I was born and suffered. For they are like a man who has a place designated for wild and untamed beasts and where he sets loose his hunting dogs and takes delight in gazing at the dogs and the wild things as they run. It is a similar case with the princes of the earth and the prelates of the churches and all the states of the world. They gaze at earthly delights with greater eagerness and pleasure than at my death and my passion and my wounds. Therefore, I shall now send them words through you; and, if they do not change their hearts and turn toward me, they will be condemned along with those who divided my clothing, and over my garments, cast lots."

(*Revelations* VII:16)

A revelation concerning the people of Cyprus

[The Lord speaks] "Now I make my complaint about the inhabitants of the kingdom of Cyprus as if about one human being. But I do not complain about my friends who dwell there and who love me with all their heart and follow my will in all things; but I speak in complaint, as if to one person, to all those who scorn me and always resist my will and so very greatly oppose me. And therefore I now speak to them all as if to one.

"O people of Cyprus, my adversary, listen and be diligently attentive to what I say to you! I have loved you as a father loves his only son, whom he has willed to exalt to all honor. I conferred on you a land in which you could have an abundance of all things necessary for the sustenance of your body. I sent to you the warmth and light of the Holy Spirit that you might understand the right Christian faith to which you faithfully bound yourself, humbly subjugating yourself to the sacred statutes and to the obedience of Holy Church. Indeed, I placed you in a place that would be quite fitting for a faithful servant, namely, among my enemies, so that in return for your earthly labors and for the physical struggle of battles you would obtain in my heavenly kingdom an even more precious crown. I also carried you for a long time in my heart, i.e., in the charity of my Godhead, and kept you as the apple of my eye in all your adversities and tribulations. And as long as you observed my precepts and faithfully kept obedience and the statutes of Holy Church, then, of a certainty, did an almost infinite number of souls come from the kingdom of Cyprus to my heavenly kingdom to enjoy eternal glory with me for ever. . . .

"Wherefore, O people of Cyprus, I now announce to you that if you will not correct yourself and amend your life, then I shall so destroy your generation and progeny in the kingdom of Cyprus that I shall spare neither the poor person nor the rich. Indeed, I shall so destroy this same generation of yours that in a short time, your memory will thus slip from the hearts of human beings as if you had never been born in this world. Afterward, however, it is my pleasure to plant new plants in the kingdom of Cyprus that will carry out my precepts and love me with all their heart. But, nevertheless, know for a certainty that if any one of you wills to correct himself, amend his life, and humbly turn back to me, then like a loving shepherd, I shall joyfully run out to meet him, lifting him onto my shoulders and personally carrying him back to my sheep. For by my shoulders I mean that if anyone amends his life, he will share in the benefit of my passion and death, which I endured in my body and shoulders; and he will receive with me eternal consolation in the kingdom of heaven."

(*Revelations* VII:19)

Concerning a bishop who was also ruler of the March of Ancona

When I, a sinner unworthy of doing so, was praying for you on the preceding day to my Lord Jesus Christ, he then appeared to me in spirit and spoke with me, using a similitude and saying this:

"O you, to whom it has been given to hear spiritually and to see, be attentive now and know for very certain that all bishops and abbots and also all the other ecclesiastical prelates and benefice-holders who have the care of souls and who leave their churches and my sheep, which have been entrusted to them, and who receive and hold other offices and positions of rulership with the intention and purpose that in these offices they may be more honored by human beings and may be exalted and raised to a higher status in the world, then, even though in those offices these rulers neither steal nor plunder anything nor commit any other injustice, nevertheless, because they glory and delight in those offices and honors and, for this reason, leave my sheep and their churches, they are, in doing these things, to my eyes like pigs dressed in pontifical or sacerdotal vestments. This situation may be expressed by means of the following similitude: There was a great lord who had invited his friends to supper. And at the hour of the supper, those pigs—dressed as above—entered into the palace in the sight of the lord and in the sight of the banqueters who sat at the table. The lord, however, wished to give to them some of those precious foods on the table; but then the aforesaid pigs cried out with a loud sound, grunting their opposition with their pig voices and refusing to eat those precious foods, although they were avidly eager to eat, in their usual way, the cheap husks meant for pigs. Then, however, when that lord saw and understood this, he loathed their vileness and filth; and at once he said to his servants with great wrath and indignation: 'Expel them from my palace and cast them forth to be refreshed and sordidly sated with the pigs' husks of which they are worthy! For they are neither willing nor worthy to eat of my foods, which have been prepared for my friends.' "

By these things, my most reverend Father and Lord, I then understood in spirit that this is what you must do: namely, that you must decide in your own conscience whether or not those sheep of Christ, namely, those entrusted to you in your bishopric, are being well and spiritually ruled in your absence. If in your absence they are being well ruled in accord with what is spiritually appropriate to their souls' advantage and benefit, and if furthermore you see that by ruling the March you can do God greater honor and be more useful to souls than in your own bishopric, then indeed I say that you can quite lawfully stay in your office as ruler of the March in accord with the will of God, provided that it is neither desire for honor nor empty glorying in that office that seduces you in staying there. If, in fact, your conscience dictates to you the contrary, then I advise you to leave the office of the marquisate and go back to reside personally in your own church and in the bishopric entrusted to you: namely, in order to rule those sheep of yours, or rather, of Christ, specially entrusted to you and to feed them by word, example and work, not negligently and faultily like a wicked hireling, but carefully and virtuously like a true and good shepherd.

Be forbearing with me, my Lord, in that I, although an ignorant woman and an unworthy sinner, write such things to you. I ask of him, our true and good Shepherd, who deigned to die for his sheep, that he may bestow on you the Holy Spirit's grace, by which you may worthily rule his sheep and always do his glorious and most holy will, even till death.

(*Revelations* VII:29)

God's judgment on the wicked

[He who sat on the throne said:] "O my enemies—abominable and ungrateful and degenerate—I seem to you, as it were, a worm dead in winter. Therefore you do whatever things you will, and you prosper. Therefore, I will arise in summer and then you shall be silent, and you shall not escape my hand. But

nevertheless, O my enemies; because I have redeemed you with
my blood and because I am in quest of naught but your souls,
therefore return to me even now with humility and I will gladly
receive you as my children. Shake off from you the devil's heavy
yoke and recall my charity, and you shall see in your conscience
that I am sweet and meek."

(*Revelations* VII:30)

Birgitta the Pilgrim

A brief resume of the Lady Birgitta's later life

The revelations in this book were received by Lady Birgitta in Rome and also when she went on pilgrimage for the first time to Naples and to Sant'Angelo on Monte Gargano. After her return and while she was in Rome, she received others that are contained here. And in that same place, it was divinely told her by Christ in a vision that she was to go overseas on a pilgrimage to the holy city of Jerusalem. Moreover, on that overseas voyage, she had very many revelations—in Naples as well as in Jerusalem and in Bethlehem—just as it had been divinely promised her beforehand. . . . After she had returned to Rome from Jerusalem, she had still others that are contained here. And then the said lady died in the City. To her, before her death, Christ foretold in a vision the time and the date on which she was to die.

(*Revelations* VII: Prologue)

A vision in Bethlehem of the birth of Christ

When I was at the manger of the Lord in Bethlehem, I saw a Virgin, pregnant and most beautiful, clothed in a white mantle and a finely woven tunic through which from without I could clearly discern her virginal flesh. Her womb was full and much swollen, for she was now ready to give birth. With her there was a very dignified old man; and with them they had both an ox and an ass. When they had entered the cave, and after the ox and the ass had been tied to the manger, the old man went outside and brought to the virgin a lighted candle and fixed it in the wall and went outside in order not to be personally present at the birth. And so the Virgin then took the shoes from her feet, put off the white mantle that covered her, removed the veil from her head, and laid these things beside her, remaining in only her tunic, with her most beautiful hair—as if of gold—spread out upon her shoulder blades. She then drew out two small cloths of linen and two of wool, very clean and finely woven, which she carried with her to wrap the infant that was to be born, and two other small linens to cover and bind his head; and she laid these cloths beside her that she might use them in due time.

And when all these things had been thus prepared, then the Virgin knelt with great reverence, putting herself at prayer; and she kept her back toward the manger and her face lifted to heaven toward the east. And so, with raised hands and with her eyes intent on heaven, she was as if suspended in an ecstasy of contemplation, inebriated with divine sweetness. And while she was thus in prayer, I saw the One lying in her womb then move; and then and there, in a moment and in the twinkling of an eye, she gave birth to a Son, from whom there went out such ineffable light and splendor that the sun could not be compared to it. Nor did that candle that the old man had put in place give light at all because that divine splendor totally annihilated the material splendor of the candle. And so sudden and momentary was that manner of giving birth that I was unable to notice or discern how or in what manner she was giving birth. But yet, at once, I saw the glorious infant lying on the earth, naked and glowing in the greatness of neatness. His flesh was most clean of all filth and uncleanness. I saw also the afterbirth, lying wrapped very neatly beside him. And then I heard the wonderfully sweet and most dulcet songs of the angels. And the Virgin's womb, which before the birth had been very swollen, at once retracted; and her body then looked wonderfully beautiful and delicate.

When therefore the Virgin felt that she had now given birth, at once, having bowed her head and joined her hands, with great dignity and reverence she adored the boy and said to him: "Welcome, my God, my Lord, and my Son!" And then the boy, crying and, as it were, trembling from the cold and the hardness of the pavement where he lay, rolled a little and extended his limbs, seeking to find refreshment and his Mother's favor. Then his Mother took him in her hands and pressed him to her breast, and with cheek and breast she warmed him with great joy and tender maternal compassion. Then, sitting on the earth, she put her Son in her lap and deftly caught his umbilical cord with her fingers. At once it was cut off, and from it no liquid or blood went out. And at once she began to wrap him carefully, first in the linen cloths and then in the woollen, binding his little body, legs, and arms with a ribbon that had been sewn into four parts of the outer woollen cloth. And afterward she wrapped and tied on the boy's head those two small linen cloths that she had prepared for this purpose. When these things therefore were accomplished, the old man entered; and prostrating on the earth, he adored him on bended knee and wept for joy. Not even at the birth was that Virgin changed in color or by infirmity. Nor was there in her any such failure of bodily strength as usually happens to other women giving birth, except that her swollen womb retracted to the prior state in which it had been before she conceived the boy. Then, however, she arose, holding the boy in her arms; and together both of them, namely, she and Joseph, put him in the manger, and on bended knee they continued to adore him with gladness and immense joy.

(*Revelations* VII:21)

A revelation in Bethlehem in the Chapel where Christ was born

The same Mother of the Lord said to me: "My daughter, know that when the three magi kings came into the stable to adore my Son, I had foreknown their coming well in advance. And when they entered and adored him, then my Son exulted, and for joy he had then a more cheerful face. I too rejoiced exceedingly; and I was gladdened by the wonderful joy of exultation in my mind, while being attentive to their words and actions, keeping those things and reflecting on them in my heart."

(*Revelations* VII:21)

Vision at Calvary (part of the Birgitta's vivid description of Christ's crucifixion)

Then too his fine and lovely eyes appeared half dead; his mouth was open and bloody; his face was pale and sunken, all livid and stained with blood; and his whole body was as if black and blue and pale and very weak from the constant downward flow of blood. Indeed, his skin and the virginal flesh of his most holy body were so delicate and tender that, after the infliction of a slight blow, a black and blue mark appeared on the surface. At times, however, he tried to make stretching motions on the cross because of the exceeding bitterness of the intense and most acute pain that he felt. For at times the pain from his pierced limbs and veins ascended to his heart and battered him cruelly with an intense martyrdom; and thus his death was prolonged and delayed amidst grave torment and great bitterness.

Then, therefore, in distress from the exceeding anguish of his pain and already near to death, he cried to the Father in a loud and tearful voice, saying: "O Father, why have you forsaken me?" He then had pale lips, a bloody tongue, with a sunken abdomen that adhered to his back as if he had no viscera within. A second time also he cried out again in the greatest pain and anxiety; 'O Father, into your hands I commend my spirit.' Then his head, raising itself a little, immediately bowed; and thus he sent forth his spirit. When his Mother saw these things, she trembled at that immense bitterness and would have fallen onto the earth if she had not been supported by the other women.

(*Revelations* VII:15)

Vision in Jerusalem at the Church of the Holy Sepulcher

The Son speaks to the bride: "When you people entered my temple, which was dedicated with my blood, you were cleansed of all your sins as if you had at that moment been lifted from the font of baptism. And because of your labors and devotion, some souls of your relatives that were in purgatory have this day been liberated and have entered into heaven in my glory. For all who come to this place with a perfect will to amend their lives in accord with their better conscience, and who are not willing to fall back into their former sins, will have all their former sins completely forgiven; and will have an increase of grace to make progress."

(Revelations VII:14)

Vision of the Virgin at the place of her Assumption into heaven

When I was in the Valley of Jehosaphat, praying at the sepulcher of the glorious Virgin, that same Virgin appeared to me, shining with exceeding splendor and said: "Be attentive, daughter! After my Son ascended to heaven, I lived in the world for fifteen years and as much more time as there is from the feast of the ascension of that same Son of mine until my death. And then I lay dead in the sepulcher for fifteen days. Thereupon I was assumed into heaven with infinite honor and joy. However, my garments with which I was buried remained in this sepulcher; and I was then clothed in such garments as those that clothe my Son and my Lord, Jesus Christ. Know also that there is no human body in heaven except the glorious body of my Son and my own body.

Therefore go now, all of you, back to the lands of Christians; ever amend your lives for the better; and in future, live with the greatest of care and attention now that you have visited these holy places, where my Son and I lived in the body and died and were buried."

(Revelations VII:26)

Prayers

Prayer in praise of the Virgin Mary

Blessed may you be, my Lady, O Virgin Mary. You were alone and ablaze with ardent love for God and—all your mind and all the strength of your powers being lifted up—you were, with ardor and diligence, contemplating the most high God to whom you had offered your virginity, when the angel was sent to you from God and, in greeting you, announced to you God's will. To him you replied most humbly, professing yourself to be God's handmaid; and then and there the Holy Spirit wonderfully filled you with all power and virtue. To you, God the Father sent his coeternal and coequal Son, who came into you then and, of your flesh and blood, took for himself a human body. Thus, at that blessed hour, the Son of God became, in you, your son, alive in his every limb and without loss of his divine majesty.

Blessed may you be, my Lady, O Virgin Mary. Of your own blessed body, the body of Christ had now been created; and in your womb you felt his body ever growing and moving, even to the time of his glorious nativity. Before anyone else, you yourself touched him with your holy hands; you wrapped him in cloths; and, in accord with the prophet's oracle, you laid him in a manger. With exultant joy, in a motherly fashion, you used the most sacred milk of your breasts to nurture him.

Glory to you, O my Lady, O Virgin Mary. While still dwelling in a contemptible house, i.e., the stable, you saw mighty kings coming to your Son from afar and humbly offering to him, with the greatest reverence, their royal guest-gifts. Afterward, with your own precious hands, you presented him in the temple; and in your blessed heart you diligently preserved all that you heard from him or saw during his infancy.

Blessed may you be, my Lady, O Virgin Mary. With your most holy offspring, you fled into Egypt; and afterward, in joy, you bore him back to Nazareth. During his physical growth you saw him, your Son, humble and obedient to yourself and to Joseph.

Blessed may you be, my Lady, O Virgin Mary. You saw your Son preaching, doing miracles, and choosing the apostles, who, being enlightened by his example, his miracles and his teaching, became witnesses of truth that your Jesus is also truly the Son of God: publishing to all nations that it was he who, through himself, had fulfilled the writings of the prophets when on behalf of the human race he patiently endured a most hard death.

Blessed may you be, my Lady, O Virgin Mary, who knew beforehand that your Son must be made captive. Later your blessed eyes with sorrow saw him bound and scourged and crowned with thorns and fixed naked to the cross with nails. You saw many despising him and calling him a traitor.

Honor be to you, my Lady, O Virgin Mary. In sorrow, you gazed at your Son as he spoke from the cross; and with your blessed ears, you dolefully heard him, in the agony of death, crying to the Father and commending his soul into his hands.

Praise to you, my Lady, O Virgin Mary. With bitter sorrow, you saw your Son hanging on the cross: from the top of his head to the soles of his feet, all black and blue and marked with the red of his own blood, and so cruelly dead. You also gazed at the bitter sight of the holes—in his feet, in his hands, and even in his glorious side. You gazed at his skin, all lacerated without mercy.

Blessed may you be, my Lady, O Virgin Mary. With tears in your eyes, you saw your Son taken down, wrapped in cloths, buried in a monument, and there guarded by soldiers.

Blessed may you be, my Lady, O Virgin Mary. To the grave intensification of your heart's deep sorrow, you parted from the sepulcher of your Son and, full of grief, were brought by his friends to the house of John. But there, at once, you felt a relief of your great sorrow because you most surely foreknew that your Son would quickly rise.

Rejoice, my most worthy Lady, O Virgin Mary, for in the same instant that your Son arose from death he willed to make this same fact known to you, his most blessed Mother. Then and there he appeared to you by himself, and later he showed to other persons that he was the one who had been raised from death after having endured death in his own living body.

Rejoice therefore, my most worthy Lady, O Virgin Mary. When death had been conquered and death's instigator had been overthrown, and heaven's entry had been opened wide through your Son, you saw him rising and triumphant with the crown of victory. And on the fortieth day after his resurrection, you saw him, in the sight of many, ascend with honor to his kingdom in heaven as himself a king accompanied by angels. . . .

Blessed may you be, O my Lady, O Virgin Mary. Every faithful creature praises the Holy Trinity for you because you are the Trinity's most worthy creature. For wretched souls you obtain prompt pardon, and for all sinners you stand forth as a most faithful advocate and proxy. Praised therefore be God, the most high Emperor and Lord, who created you for such great honor that you yourself became both Empress and Lady everlastingly in the kingdom of heaven, forever to reign with him unto ages of ages. Amen.

(Prayers)

In praise of Christ

Blessed may you be, my Lord, my God, and my Love most beloved of my soul: O you who are one God in three Persons.

Glory and praise to you, my Lord Jesus Christ. You were sent by the Father into the body of a virgin; and yet you ever remain with the Father in heaven, while the Father, in his divinity, inseparably remained with you in your human nature in this world.

Honor and glory be to you, my Lord Jesus Christ. After having been conceived by the power of the Holy Spirit, you physically grew in the Virgin's womb; and in it you humbly dwelt until the time of your birth. After your delightful nativity, you deigned to be touched by the most clean hands of your Mother, to be wrapped in cloths, and to be laid in a manger.

Blessed may you be, my Lord Jesus Christ. You willed that your immaculate flesh be circumcised and that you be called Jesus. You willed to be offered by your Mother in the temple.

Blessed may you be, my Lord Jesus Christ. You had yourself baptized in the Jordan by your servant John.

Blessed may you be, my Lord Jesus Christ. With your blessed mouth, you preached to human beings the words of life; and in their sight, through yourself, within your actual presence, you worked many miracles.

Blessed may you be, my Lord Jesus Christ. By fulfilling the writings of the prophets, you manifested to the world in a rational way that you are the true God.

Blessing and glory be to you, my Lord Jesus Christ. For forty days you wonderfully fasted in the desert. You permitted yourself to be tempted by your enemy, the devil, whom—when it so pleased you—you drove from yourself with a single word.

Blessed may you be, my Lord Jesus Christ. You foretold your death ahead of time. At the last supper, of material bread you wonderfully consecrated your precious Body, and charitably bestowed it upon the apostles in memory of your most worthy passion. By washing their feet with your own precious and holy hands, you humbly showed your very great humility.

Honor be to you, my Lord Jesus Christ. In fear of suffering and death, you gave forth from your innocent body blood in the place of sweat. Nonetheless, you accomplished for us the redemption that you had willed to perform; and thus you manifestly showed the charity that you had toward the human race. . . .

Blessed my you be, my Lord Jesus Christ. Most patiently in Pilate's presence, with your own blessed ears you willed to hear abuse and lies hurled at you, and the voices of the people asking that the guilty robber be acquitted and that you, the innocent, be condemned.

Honor to you, my Lord Jesus Christ. With your glorious body covered in gore, the judgment on you was the death of the cross. The cross you bore in pain on your sacred shoulders; and, amidst frenzy, you were led to the place of your passion. Despoiled of your garments, thus you willed to be fixed to the wood of the cross.

Glory unmeasured to you, my Lord Jesus Christ. For us you humbly endured that [they] . . . stretched out your venerable hands and feet with rope, that they cruelly fixed them with iron nails to the wood of the cross, that they called you a traitor, that in manifold ways they derided you with unspeakable words, while above you was inscribed that title of confusion.

Eternal praise and thanksgiving to you, my Lord Jesus Christ. With what great meekness you suffered for us such cruel sorrows! On the cross your blessed body was emptied of all its strength; your kindly eyes grew dark; as your blood decreased a pallor covered all your comely face; your blessed tongue grew swollen, hot and dry; your mouth dripped from the bitter drink; your hair and beard were filled with blood from the wounds of your most holy head; the bones of your hands, of your feet, and of all your precious body were dislocated from their sockets to your great and intense grief; the veins and nerves of all your blessed body were cruelly broken; you were so monstrously scourged and so injured with painful wounds that your most innocent flesh and skin were intolerably lacerated. Thus afflicted and aggrieved, you, O my most sweet Lord, stood on the cross, and, with patience and humility, awaited in extreme pain the hour of your death.

Perpetual honor be to you, Lord Jesus Christ. Placed in this your anguish, with your most kind and charitable eyes you humbly looked upon your most worthy Mother, who never sinned nor gave to the slightest sin any consent. While consoling her who was your own, you committed her to the faithful keeping of your disciple.

Eternal blessing to you, my Lord Jesus Christ. In the agony of death you gave to all sinners the hope of forgiveness, when to the robber who had turned to you, you mercifully promised the glory of paradise.

Eternal praise to you, my Lord Jesus Christ, for each and every hour that you endured such great bitterness and anguish on the cross for us sinners. For the most acute pains proceeding from your wounds direly penetrated your happy soul and cruelly passed through your most sacred heart until your heart cracked and you happily sent forth your spirit, and with bowed head humbly commending it to the hands of God your Father. Then, having died in the body, you remained there cold.

Blessed may you be, my Lord Jesus Christ. By your precious blood and by your most sacred death, you redeemed souls and mercifully led them back from exile to eternal life. . . .

Blessed may you be, and praiseworthy and glorious unto the ages, my Lord Jesus. You sit upon the throne in your kingdom of heaven, in the glory of your divinity, corporeally alive, with all your most holy limbs that you took from the flesh of the Virgin. Even thus shall you come on the day of judgment to judge the souls of all the living and the dead: you who live and reign with the Father and the Holy Spirit unto ages of ages. Amen.

(Prayers)

Praise of the heart of Christ

My Lord Jesus Christ, your blessed, royal, and magnificent heart could never, by torments or terror or blandishments, be swayed from the defense of your kingdom of truth and justice. You did not spare your most worthy body in any way; but rather, with your magnificent heart, you faithfully strove for justice and the law and intrepidly preached to your friends and to your enemies the law's precepts and the counsels of perfection. By dying in battle to defend these things, you—and your holy followers with you—have obtained the victory. Therefore, it is right that your unconquered heart be ever magnified in heaven and on earth and be unceasingly praised with triumphal honor by all creatures and soldiers. Amen

(Prayers)

Birgitta's Death

Christ foretells Birgitta's passing

It happened five days before the passing of Lady Birgitta, the often-mentioned bride of Christ, that our Lord Jesus Christ appeared to her in front of the altar that stood in her chamber. He showed himself with a joyful face and said to her: "I have done to you what a bridegroom usually does, concealing himself from his bride so that he might be the more ardently desired by her. Thus I have not visited you with consolations during this time; for it was the time of your testing. Therefore, now that you have already been tested, go forward and prepare yourself; for now is the time for the fulfillment of that which I promised you: namely, that before my altar you shall be clothed and consecrated as a nun. And henceforth you shall be counted, not only as my bride, but also a nun and a mother in Vadstena. Nevertheless, know that you will lay down your body here in Rome until it comes to the place prepared for it. For it pleases me to spare you from your labors and to accept your will in place of the completed action." . . .

"On the morning of the fifth day, after you have received the sacraments, call together one by one the persons who are present and living with you and whom I have just now named to you, and tell them the things they must do. And thus, amidst these words and their hands, you will come to your monastery, i.e., into my joy; and your body will be placed in Vadstena." Then, as the fifth day approached, at the moment of dawn, Christ appeared to her again and consoled her. But when Mass had been said and after she had received the sacraments with very great devotion and reverence, in the hands of the aforesaid persons she sent forth her spirit.

(*Revelations* VII:31)

Julian of Norwich

1342–1420

Introduction

Julian is the only woman in this book who has not been officially canonized or beatified by the Roman Catholic Church. This could be due to the fact that her writings have only recently been published for a general readership, and she is too far away in time for us to know much about her life; but that does not mean that she is not a teacher of note who seems to have a special message of hope for today's world.

Julian (we do not even know her real name, for she was an anchoress attached to the church of Saint Julian in Norwich, and most likely adopted that name as her own in later life) was born in England in 1342. It was a time of tragedy and unrest. England was in the midst of the Thirty Years war with France. The plague ravished the city of Norwich when Julian was six and again when she was nineteen. More than half the population died, and the town was filled with heaps of stinking bodies. People were too terrified to bury the dead lest they too should succumb to the dreaded sickness. Great pits were dug and the corpses hastily interred at night. Scarcely a family remained untouched by the tragedy.

We can presume that Julian grew to womanhood in that era when childhood was short and somber. In the process she would need to learn all the familiar domestic tasks that fell to a woman's lot: sewing, weaving, cooking, household management, candle making, food preserving. Most probably Julian was either married at the usual age and later left a widow, or remained a dedicated single woman after the manner of a beguine. There is no mention in her book of religious life or of the spirituality associated with nuns of the time.

Julian was a deeply religious person touched early by death and sorrow. Like many before and since, she had turned to the Crucified for solace, but unlike others she herself tells us that she had begged for three specific gifts in the process. The first was an experience of the passion, as if she had been actually present on Calvary; the second was for a near-death encounter at the age of thirty; the third request was for the gift of three wounds, which she saw as integral to the Christian life as she understood it—the wounds of contrition, natural compassion, and longing for God. While the third request remained in Julian's consciousness as a continual prayer, she forgot about the other two requests until they actually came to pass in the spring of her thirty-first year.

In early May 1373, Julian found herself prostrated by some kind of mortal illness. She lay in great pain, her body slowly succumbing to creeping paralysis. A priest came to administer the Last Rites, while her mother stood nearby waiting to close her daughter's eyes. Then suddenly Julian remembered her request for a deeper experience of the passion; she had asked for it in faith, and before her eyes the crucifix began to bleed. This was the beginning of a remarkable two days, during which time Julian received what she termed a "Revelation of Love" comprising sixteen *Showings* (or insights) revolving around the love of Christ, and incorporating the great themes of redemption, mercy, God's providence, the mystery of sin, and the most famous of all her insights—that, while sin is part of the picture in all our lives and in the history of the world at large, in the end "All shall be well, and all manner of things shall be well."

It was most likely some time after this that Julian retired to an anchorhold in order to ponder on all that had been revealed to her in those few packed hours when she hovered between life and death. In pondering and writing she has been acknowledged as a true theologian. Unlike the other women in this book she did not have a series of ongoing revelations. Instead she penetrated ever more deeply into the one revelation she was given, dividing it into sixteen parts, and in each part examining the mysteries of God's love as revealed in the mystery of Christ's cross, the Trinity, and other related topics. Some of her insights are both remarkable and unique, for example her writings on Christ as mother, and in her insistence that God is not, and cannot be, angry with us on any account. She holds in tension many of the great themes of Christianity—sin and forgiveness, mercy and judgment, evil and God's all-encompassing compassion. She is a prophet of hope for a world sunk in despair. She finds God in the metaphors of ordinary life: in feeding and birthing, in knitting and attending to bodily needs, in herring scales and a cloth in the wind. Her theology is Trinitarian and Christo-centric. She has the confidence to hold to her insights even when they seem to run counter to orthodox Christian teaching such as the damnation of sinners. She acknowledges that she can only see a part of the picture, but she holds to what God has "shown" her with sensitivity and respect for other views.

The solitary life which Julian chose to follow, and in which she perse-vered into her seventies (in those days a great age) could be embraced either by professed religious—monks and nuns—or by lay people, though evidence suggests that in the fourteenth century lay people predominated. Men who became hermits could, if they wished, live in the open countryside, perhaps serving the local populace by keeping roads and bridges in repair and offering hospitality to the occasional wayfarer. Women on the other hand were expected to remain "anchored" in one place, safe beside a church or convent.

While the rule of enclosure was strictly adhered to and an anchoress could not leave her designated domain, life within it was relatively balanced and humane. Food was supposed to be nourishing and well served. Cleanliness was encouraged and all harsh penances eschewed. This was not the life of the desert fathers but of tempered asceticism. Prayers were recited at set times during the day, but books were few, as these were for the most part secreted in monastic libraries.

Julian's anchorhold was situated in the midst of Norwich's commer-cial area. From it she would be expected to counsel others, listen to their sorrows, pray for those around her and be available in other ways commensurate with her enclosure. She would be expected to earn her living by sewing or other handwork, for she had to provide both for herself and a maid who would run errands and liaise with the outside world. In addition, a single woman might well have some form of fixed income provided by her family or have alms left for her upkeep in bequests and wills. Far from being apart from society, a city anchoress was in many ways more deeply immersed in its heart; more so than a nun of the same period.

Meanwhile, during her years of reclusion Julian found time to write or dictate her *Showings* and the meaning she was discovering in them. She terms herself "unlettered" and most likely she was such by university standards. There was little schooling available then for women; most could neither read nor write, and even nuns recited the Office from memory. Either Julian taught herself in order to communicate her insights, or she dictated to a scribe. The former seems more probable as the finished book has many cross-references; and also long periods spent with a scribe would be frowned upon as giving cause for scandal. So Julian wrote. She wrote the first spiritual treatise ever in the language of the common people—not French, not Latin, but in a tongue still newly born, with its particular richness and rhythm. Julian, though "unlettered" produced a masterpiece. There is nothing to compare with it, for it is unique. Julian is the acknowledged "first lady" of written English.

So what happened to Julian's book? Why has it only come to light recently? Unlike most of the continental mystics Julian belonged to no Order which might cherish her memory and disseminate her writings. Nor had she a devout following such as the "spiritual sons and daughters" of Angela of Foligno. She was not known as an ecstatic or mystic by the general populace. The only contemporary mention of Julian is by Margery Kempe who visited her and sought her counsel as a wise woman in the ways of the spirit, but there is no mention of her being a visionary. Her life within the anchorhold was similar to that of any solitary woman. There were no levitations, no further visions, no inspired heavenly pronouncements. Her *Showings* lasted a few hours, and for the rest of her life she had to live, like most of us, by faith not sight—praying, pondering, questioning, sifting, penetrating the mystery of Christ and his redeeming work.

Julian's book was the work of a single obscure anchoress. It was not in the ecclesiastical language of the time and most of the hand-written copies available were no doubt destroyed when the monasteries were dissolved. Of the two remaining copies one was cherished on continental Europe by English Catholic refugees. However, for the most part pre-Reformation English spirituality was unexplored territory.

In 1901 a previously unknown and untaught scholar, Grace Warrack, discovered an edition of Julian in the British Library and brought out a new translation. Suddenly people awoke to the fact that here was a woman who had something to say to contemporary society, and many other translations and commentaries quickly followed. A shorter version of Julian's book was also discovered, seemingly written shortly after her initial experience, and well before the longer book which contained the fruit of many years' meditation.

Julian seems to have been kept for today, fresh and inspiring, a voice of joy and optimism, yet also a powerful prober of life's ultimate questions. She is a true searcher after God, fully committed, original in her thinking, traditional in her Christian devotion, courageous in exploring, stable in her radical commitment to solitude—a solitude in which she held, with love, all her fellow-Christians. From being voiceless and unknown Julian is now acclaimed. Thomas Merton, the well-known Cistercian monk, admitted that he would prefer Julian to John of the cross, calling her, together with Newman, the greatest theologian England has produced. It is this theology which appeals; a theology rooted in daily life and experience. Julian is not a mere "descriptive" visionary. She penetrates the *meaning* of the Christian mystery and elucidates it in an inimitable and original way.

In this volume I have used the translation by Joseph Pichler of the Paris manuscript of the Long Text of Julian's *Revelations*, grouping my choice of extracts around some of her main themes. I am grateful to Rev. Pichler for allowing me free use of his unpublished manuscript for my work, and permitting me to edit his text where necessary.

The Background to Julian's Revelations

Julian's three desires

This creature had previously desired three gifts by the grace of God. The first was recollection of the passion. The second was physical sickness at the young age of thirty. The third was to receive three wounds as God's gift.

As far as the first goes, I thought I had already experienced something of the passion of Christ; yet by the grace of God I desired still more. I wished I had really been there with Mary Magdalene and the others who loved him, in order to see with my own eyes the passion that our Lord suffered for me, and so be able to suffer with him, as was granted to those who loved him and were near to him. For this reason I wanted to have a bodily vision through which I could understand better the physical pains of our Lord, and the compassion of Our Lady, and of all his true lovers alive at the time who saw his pains. I wanted to have been one of them and have suffered with them. Apart from this I never had any other desire of a vision or revelation from God until my soul would depart from the body, for I believed I would be saved by the mercy of God. The reason for this prayer was that after the vision I might more truly understand the passion of Christ.

With regard to the second gift: it came to my mind with contrition, freely and without seeking it. It was an intense desire to have from God the gift of a physical illness. I wanted this illness to be severe even to the point of death so that I could receive all the rites of Holy Church, I myself being convinced that I would die, and that also all others who saw me would think the same. I did not want to have any kind of comfort that earthly life can offer. I wanted to have all the different pains, physical and spiritual, that I would have had had I really died, with all the fears and temptations of the devil, and every other kind of pain except the actual departure of my soul. I desired this because I wanted to be fully cleansed by the mercy of God, and afterward, as a result of this sickness, live a more consecrated life for the glory of God. I hoped that this would be to my advantage after my death, for I desired soon to be with my God and Maker.

These two desires, for the passion and for the sickness, I asked God for conditionally, because it seemed to me that this was not the ordinary practice of prayer. Therefore I said: "Lord, you know what I want. If it is your will, let me have it. But if it is not your will good Lord, do not be angry, for I want nothing that is not your will."

As for the third gift, by the grace of God and the teaching of Holy Church, I developed a strong desire to receive three wounds during my life: that is to say, the wound of true contrition, the wound of natural compassion, and the wound of unshakeable longing for God. And as I prayed for the other two gifts conditionally, so I prayed for this third one without condition.

The first two desires I soon forgot, but the third remained with me continually.

(Revelations 2)

The Crucified Christ

Julian's first vision of the Crucified

Immediately I saw the red blood trickle down from under the garland of thorns, a living stream of hot, fresh blood, just as it was at the time of his passion when the crown of thorns was pressed on his blessed head. And I saw very clearly and power-fully that the God-man who suffered for me was the very same one who showed this vision to me without any go-between.

And in the same vision, the Trinity suddenly filled my heart with the deepest joy. I immediately realized that this will be the permanent experience of those who go to heaven. For the Trinity is God. God is the Trinity. The Trinity is our maker, the Trinity is our keeper, the Trinity is our everlasting lover. The Trinity is our everlasting joy and bliss, through our Lord Jesus Christ and in our Lord Jesus Christ. And this was shown to me in the first reve-lation and in all the others; for wherever Jesus appears, the whole Blessed Trinity is to be understood, as I see it.

(*Revelations* 4)

Description of Christ's bleeding head

During the whole time that our Lord showed me this spiritual vision which I have just described, I saw with my bodily eyes the head of Christ continuously and heavily bleeding. The great drops of blood fell down from under the crown like pellets, which looked as if they had come from the veins. When they came out they were of a brownish-red color (for the blood was very thick), and as they spread they were bright red. Then when they reached the eyebrows they vanished. Yet the bleeding continued until I had seen and understood many things. Nevertheless, the beautiful and lifelike head continued in the same beauty and vividness without diminishing.

The abundance was like the drops of water that fall off the eaves of a roof after a heavy shower of rain, falling so thickly that it is beyond human skill to count them. And as they spread out on the forehead they were as round as a herring's scales.

These three images came to my mind at that time: pellets, because of the roundness of the drops of blood when they first appeared; herring scales because of the roundness spreading on the forehead; raindrops falling from the eaves because they were too many to count.

This vision was real and lifelike, horrifying and fearful, sweet and lovely. And what gave me most encouragement in the whole vision was the knowledge that our good Lord, who is so holy and fearful, is also homely and courteous. And it is this that filled my soul with delight and assurance. . . .

It seems to me that the greatest joy we shall ever know comes from seeing the wonderful courtesy and homeliness of our Father who is our Creator; and we see it in our Lord Jesus Christ, who is our brother and savior.

(*Revelations* 7)

The saving power of the blood of Christ

After this I saw the body bleeding heavily, apparently from the scourging. The smooth skin was gashed with furrows which penetrated deep into the tender flesh because of the many sharp blows inflicted all over that sweet body. The hot blood flowed out heavily, so that neither the wounds nor the skin could be seen, but all seemed to be covered in blood.

And when it came to the place where it should have fallen down it vanished. Nevertheless, the bleeding still continued for some time so that I could clearly observe it with attention. It was so heavy that I thought that if it had been real and genuine blood at that moment, the whole bed and everything around would have been soaked in blood. Then the idea came to me that, out of the tender love God has for us, he has created a vast supply of water on earth for our use and bodily comfort. Yet he much prefers that we take for our perfect cure his blessed blood to wash ourselves clean of sin; for there has been no liquid made which he would prefer to give us. It is most plentiful as it is most precious, and that by virtue of his blessed Godhead. It is of our own nature, and blessedly flows over us by the power of his precious love.

The priceless blood of our Lord Jesus Christ is truly plentiful as it is most precious. Behold and see the power of this precious abundance of his priceless blood. It descended down to hell, burst hell's chains and freed all who were there who belonged to the court of heaven. The precious abundance of his priceless blood flows over the whole world, ready to wash away all sin from every human being who is of good will, who has been and shall be. The precious abundance of his priceless blood rises up to heaven in the blessed body of our Lord Jesus Christ; and there it is now with him, bleeding and praying for us to the Father. That is how it is now, and shall be as long as we have need of it. And even more, it flows through all heaven, rejoicing at the salvation of all people who are already there and who are still to come, thus completing the appointed number of all the saints.

(*Revelations* 12)

"I chose Jesus for my heaven"

At that time I wanted to look away from the cross but I dared not, because I knew quite well that while I gazed at the cross I was secure and safe. Therefore I did not want to give in to the desire and put my soul in danger, for apart from the cross there was no safety from the terror of demons.

Then a suggestion was put into my mind in an apparently friendly manner: "Look up to heaven to his Father." With the faith I had I saw clearly that there was nothing between the cross and heaven that could have harmed me. I had therefore either to look up or refuse to do so. I answered inwardly with all the power of my soul saying: "No, I cannot, for you are my heaven." I said this because I did not want to look up. I would rather have remained in that pain until judgment day than enter heaven in any other way than through him. I knew very well that he who bound me so painfully would unbind me when he wished.

In this way I was taught to choose Jesus for my heaven, whom I saw only in pain at that time. I wanted no other heaven than Jesus, who will be my bliss when I get there.

It has always been a great comfort to me that by his grace I chose Jesus for my heaven throughout all this time of his passion and sorrow. This has taught me that I should always do so, choosing only Jesus to be my heaven through thick and thin.

(*Revelations* 19)

The joy of Christ

Our good Lord asked me: "Are you well satisfied that I suffered for you?" I said "Yes, good Lord, and I thank you very much. Yes, good Lord, may you be blessed." Then Jesus, our good Lord, said: "If you are satisfied then I am satisfied. To have ever suffered the passion for you is for me a great joy, a bliss, and endless delight; and if I could suffer more I would do so. . . ."

And in these words: "If I could suffer more I would do so" I saw truly that as often as he could die he would die, and love would never let him rest until he had done it.

(*Revelations* 22)

"See how much I love you"

With a joyful expression our good Lord looked at his wounded side and contemplated it with joy. And with his sweet gaze he led the understanding of this creature through the same wound into his side, right inside it. And there he showed me a beautiful and enjoyable place, big enough to contain all who shall be saved, that they might rest there in peace and in love. And with this he brought to my mind his priceless blood and the precious water which he allowed to flow out for love of us.

In this sweet contemplation he showed me his blessed heart cloven in two; and with great delight he showed partially to my understanding the blessed Godhead (as far as he wanted at that moment), strengthening in this way the poor soul to understand that which cannot be expressed in words—the endless love which was without beginning, is, and ever shall be.

And with this our good Lord said most blissfully: "See how much I love you." As if he had said: "My dear one, behold and see your Lord, your God, who is your Creator and your endless joy. See your own brother, your Savior. My child, behold and see what delight and bliss I have in your salvation, and for my love, rejoice now with me."

And further, in order to have a still deeper understanding, this blessed word was said: "See how much I love you." It was as if he had said: "Behold and see that I loved you so much before I died for you that I was willing to die for you. Now I have died for you, and suffered willingly what I could, and now all my bitter pains and all my hard turmoil have changed into endless joy and bliss for me and for you. How should it be that you should now ask me for anything that pleases me and I should not give it to you with pleasure. For my pleasure is your holiness and your endless joy and bliss with me."

This is the understanding, as simply as I can put it, of this blessed word: "See how much I love you." This has been shown to me by our good Lord in order to make us glad and happy.

(*Revelations* 24)

The dying Christ

I looked with bodily sight into the face of the crucifix before me. There I saw part of Christ's passion: contempt, disgusting spittle, buffeting, and many long drawn out pains, more than I can tell. His color often changed as I watched. At one time half his face, beginning at the ear, became covered with dried blood, until it reached the middle of his face. Then the other side became caked with blood in the same manner. Meanwhile the blood vanished on the other side just as it had come.

This I saw dimly, and I wanted more light so as to see better. And I was answered in my reason: "If God wants to show you more he will be light for you. You need no other light except him." For I saw him and I sought him; indeed we are now so blind and foolish that we can never seek God until that time when God shows himself to us in his goodness. And when by grace we see something of him, then we are moved by the same grace to seek with greater desire and with greater joy. So I saw him and I sought him. I had him and I lacked him. And this is how we generally are in this life, as I see it.

(*Revelations* 10)

Accept my vision as if shown to you personally

Everything that I am saying about myself I mean to say about all my fellow-Christians, for I was taught in the spiritual vision that this is what our Lord intends it for. Therefore, I beg you all, for God's sake, and I advise you for your own benefit, that you stop thinking about the poor wretch to whom the vision was shown, and that you better, powerfully, wisely and humbly contemplate God himself who, in his courteous love and his endless goodness, wanted to show these things to all so that all might be comforted. It is God's will that you accept it with the greatest joy and delight as if Jesus himself had shown it to *you*.

I am not good because of this vision, but only if I love God more because of it. And to the extent that you love God more than I do, you are that much better than I am. I am not saying this to those who are wise, for they know it well enough. But I am saying it to you who are simple, to give you peace and comfort, for we are in fact all one in love. And truly it was not shown to me that God loves me more than the least soul that is in a state of grace. I am sure that there are many who never had any revelations or visions outside the ordinary teaching of Holy Church and yet who love God more than I do.

If I look at myself alone I am nothing at all, but in the whole body of Christ I am, I hope, united in love with all my fellow-Christians. It is on this union of love that the life of all those who are going to be saved depends. For God is all that is good (as I see it) and God has made all that is made and loves all that is made.

Therefore, whoever loves fellow-Christians as a whole for God's sake, loves all that is made. For in humankind that shall be saved everything is understood as being present: I mean all that is made, and the Maker of all. For God is in us, and God is in all. And whoever loves thus, loves all. And I hope, by the grace of God, that whoever sees things in this way shall be truly taught and mightily comforted, if in need of comfort.

(*Revelations* 8, 9)

The Visions of Our Lady

Mary, the young girl

Then he brought our Lady, Saint Mary, to my attention. I saw her spiritually in bodily likeness, a simple, humble maiden, young in years and little more than a child, in the form in which she was when she conceived. God showed me something of the wisdom and truth of her soul, and through this I understood her sense of reverence with which she beheld God, her Creator. I also understood her profound, wondering reverence, that he, her Creator, should want to be born of her, someone so simple and of his own making. This wisdom and truth, this knowledge of her Creator's greatness and her own littleness as creature, made her say to Gabriel in deep humility: "Behold me here, God's handmaiden." In this vision I understood without any doubt that, as far as worthiness and wholeness are concerned, she is superior to everything else that God has made; for above her there is nothing in the created order except Jesus Christ in his humanity, as I see it.

(*Revelations* 4)

The compassion of our Lady

Here I saw something of the compassion of our Lady Saint Mary, for Christ and she were so one in love that the greatness of her love was the cause of the greatness of her pain. In this I saw the substance of natural love developed by grace which his creatures have for him. This natural love was most supremely and sweetly shown in his sweet mother. For inasmuch as she loved him more than all others, her pain surpassed all others. For always the higher, the stronger, the sweeter love is, the greater is the sorrow of the one who sees the body of their beloved suffer. So all his disciples and all his true lovers suffered far more when he suffered than when they themselves died. I am sure, from the way I feel myself, that the very least of them loved him so much more than they loved themselves that I am unable to put it into words.

(*Revelations* 18)

See in Mary how much you are loved

With this same expression of mirth and joy our good Lord looked down to his right side and brought to my mind where our Lady stood at the time of his passion, and he said: "Would you like to see her?" and this sweet word sounded as if he had said: "I know quite well that you would like to see my blessed Mother, because after myself she is the highest joy that I could show you. She is the greatest pleasure and honor to me, and the one whom all my blessed creatures most desire to see." And because of the unique, exalted and wonderful love that he has for this sweet maiden, his blessed Mother our Lady Saint Mary, he showed her bliss and her joy through this sweet word, as if he said: "Would you like to see how I love her, so that you can rejoice with me in the love that I have for her and she for me."

And also to understand this sweet word better, our good Lord speaks in love to all people who are to be saved as if they were one single person. By this he seemed to say: "Do you want to see in her how much you are loved? It is for love of you that I have created her so exalted, so noble, so worthy, and this pleases me. And I wish that you too are pleased with it." For after himself she is the most blissful sight. But here I was not taught that I should long to see her physical presence whilst I am here on earth, but rather to seek the virtues of her blessed soul: her truth, her wisdom, her love, through which I know myself and reverently fear God.

And when our good Lord had shown me this and said the word "Do you want to see her?" I answered and said: "Yes, good Lord. Thanks be to you, good Lord. Yes, good Lord if it be your will." I said this prayer many times and I expected to see her in bodily likeness, but I did not see her so. And Jesus showed me in this word a spiritual sight of her.

And just as I had seen her before little and simple, so he showed her to me now exalted, noble and glorious, and more pleasing to him than all creatures. And so he wants it to be known that all who take delight in him should also take delight in her, and rejoice in the delight that he has in her and she in him.

(*Revelations* 25)

Teaching on Prayer

God's love for us and for all creation

At the same time as I had the bodily vision of the bleeding head, our good Lord also gave me a spiritual vision of his homely loving. I saw that he is everything that is good and comfortable for our help. He is our clothing which for love enwraps us and enfolds us, embraces us and fully shelters us; and with his tender love he is so close to us that he can never leave us. So I saw in this vision that he is everything that is good, as far as I could understand.

Then he showed me a little thing, no bigger than a hazelnut as it seemed to me, lying in the palm of my hand. I looked at it with the eye of my understanding and thought: "What can this be?" And I was answered generally: "It is all that is made." I gazed with astonishment, wondering how it could survive because of its littleness. It seemed to me that it should presently fall into nothingness. And I was answered in my mind: "It lasts and always will last because God loves it." And so everything receives its being from the love of God.

In this little thing I saw three truths: the first is that God made it; the second is that God loves it; the third is that God keeps it. But what did I really see? In truth I saw the Creator, the Lover, and the Keeper. For until I am substantially united to him I can never have perfect rest and true happiness. I mean to say, that I must be so united to him that no created thing can come between my God and me.

This little thing, it seemed to me, could have fallen into nothingness because of its littleness. We need to be aware of the littleness of created things in order to avoid being attached to them, and so come to love and possess God who is uncreated.

For this is the reason why we are not fully at ease in heart and soul. We seek rest in insignificant things which can offer us no rest, and we do not know our God who is all-powerful, totally wise and good. He alone is true rest. God wishes to be known by us, and he delights when we rest in him. For all that is less than him is not enough for us. This is the reason why no soul can be at rest until it is emptied of all created things. When the soul voluntarily and for love lets go of all created things in order to possess him who is all, then it is able to receive spiritual rest.

Our good Lord also showed me that it gives him great pleasure when a helpless soul comes to him openly, plainly and humbly. From this vision I understood that the soul naturally longs to do this through the touch of the Holy Spirit, saying:

> God, of your goodness give me yourself,
> for you are enough for me.
> I can ask nothing less if I am truly to live for your glory.
> If I were to ask less I would always remain in need.
> Only in you have I all.

These words of God's goodness are very dear to the soul and most nearly touching the will of our Lord. For his goodness fills all his creatures and all his blessed works, and surpasses them without end. For he himself is the Eternal, and he made us for himself alone, and restored us by his most blessed passion, and is always keeping us safe in his blessed love. All this is the work of his goodness.

(*Revelations* 5)

Knowing God's goodness, the highest form of prayer

To center on the goodness of God is the highest form of prayer, and God's goodness comes to meet us at our most basic need. It gives life to our soul and makes it live and grow in virtue and grace. It is the nearest to us by nature and the readiest to bring us grace; for it is the same grace the soul seeks and ever will seek, until the day in which we truly know God who has completely enfolded us in himself.

A person goes upright and any food eaten is preserved in the body as in a most beautiful purse. When it is necessary, the purse opens, and then it is shut again in full honesty. And that it is God who does this is shown where he says that he comes down to the lowest part of our need. For he does not despise what he has made, nor does he disdain to serve us even in the simplest of our natural bodily functions, for he loves the soul that he has made in his own likeness.

For just as the body is clothed in clothes, and flesh in the skin, and the bones in the flesh, and the heart in the whole, so are we, body and soul, clad and enclosed in the goodness of God. Yes, and even more intimately, because all these other things may wear out and vanish, but the goodness of God is always whole and close to us without compare.

Truly our Lover desires our soul to cling to him with all its might and to cling evermore to his goodness. For of all the things the heart could think of, this pleases God most and soonest helps the soul to prayerfulness. Our soul is so preciously loved by him who is highest that it is far beyond the comprehension of all creatures. That is to say, no created being can fully know how much, how sweetly, and how tenderly our Creator loves us. And therefore we can, with his grace and his help, remain in spiritual contemplation, endlessly marvelling at the high, surpassing, immeasurable love, which our Lord in his goodness has for us. So we may reverently ask from our Lord all that we want; for our natural will is to have God, and the good will of our Lord is to have us.

We can never stop wanting to be his, and longing for him, until we possess him in the fulness of joy; then we will desire nothing more. He wants us to be completely occupied with knowing and loving him until the time when our longing shall be completely fulfilled in heaven. For of all things, the beholding and loving of the Creator makes the soul seem less in its own eyes, and fills it fully with reverent fear and true humility, and with abundant love for our fellow Christians.

(*Revelations* 6)

Persevering in trust

At one time my mind was led down to the bottom of the sea, and there I saw hills and green valleys seeming as if they were covered with moss, seaweed and gravel. Then I understood this to mean that, even if a man or woman were under deep water, they would be safe in body and soul and come to no harm if they could see God who is with us all the time. And moreover, they would have more consolation and comfort than all this world can tell. For God wills that we believe that we see him all the time, even though the seeing is very little. And in this faith he makes us grow ever more in grace; because he wants to be seen and he wants to be sought; he wants to be awaited and he wants to be trusted.

(*Revelations* 10)

Three gifts for seeking God

It is the will of God that we have in our seeking three things as a gift from him.

The first is that we seek willingly and diligently, without sloth, as far as we can through his grace; gladly and happily, without unreasonable sadness and useless sorrow.

The second is that we wait for him steadfastly, out of love for him, without grumbling or striving against him until our life's end (which cannot be far away).

The third is that we trust him utterly out of complete faith in him. For he wants us to know that he will appear suddenly and blessedly to all who love him.

His work is done in secret, yet he wants to be perceived, and his appearing will be very sudden. And he wants to be trusted, for he is so homely and courteous.

Blessed may he be!

(*Revelations* 10)

God wants us to pray always

Praying is a true, gracious and lasting will of the soul, united and fastened to the will of our Lord by the sweet inner work of the Holy Spirit. Our Lord himself is the first to receive our prayer, as I see it, and he accepts it with great thankfulness and with great rejoicing. He raises it up and places it in his treasure-house where it will never perish. It is there before God with all his holy saints, furthering our cause. And when we shall receive our bliss, our prayer will be given back to us as an extra joy, with endless praise and thanks from him.

Our Lord is very happy and glad with our prayer. He expects it and he wants to have it, because with his grace it makes us as like himself in condition as we are in nature. This is his blessed will, for he says: "Pray wholeheartedly, even though you do not feel like it; for it is a very profitable thing to do, even if you do not feel that way inclined. Pray wholeheartedly, even when you may feel nothing, even when you see nothing, yes, even when you think you cannot do it. For in times of dryness and barrenness, in times of sickness and weakness, your prayer is most pleasing to me, even though you may find it rather tasteless. And this holds good in my eyes for all your prayer said in faith. . . ."

Thanksgiving is also an integral part of prayer. Thanksgiving is a true inward awareness. With deep reverence and loving fear it leads us to turn with all our strength to the work the Lord is calling us to do, all the time rejoicing and thanking him in our hearts.

Sometimes the soul is so full that it overflows into words and cries out: "Good Lord, thanks be to you, may you be blessed!" And sometimes, when the heart is dry and feels nothing, or else, when attacked by the enemy, then reason and grace drive us to cry aloud to the Lord, recounting his blessed passion and his great goodness. Then the power of our Lord's word enters the soul, enlivens the heart, leads it by his grace into true working, causes it to pray with utter happiness and truly delight in our Lord. This is for him a most loving thanksgiving.

(*Revelations* 41)

Prayer and trust

This is our Lord's will—that our prayer and our trust be both equally great. If our trust is not as great as our prayer then we do not fully honor our Lord in our prayer. Further, we hinder and hurt ourselves. The reason for this is, I believe, that we do not truly know that our Lord is the ground from which our prayer springs forth, and also that we do not know that it is given to us by grace out of his love. If we knew this we would surely be inspired to trust that our Lord would gift us with all the things that we desire.

I am quite sure that no one asks for mercy and grace with right intention unless mercy and grace have been given first. But sometimes we think that we have prayed for a long time and yet it seems that we have not been granted our request. However, we should not allow this to depress us, for I am sure that our good Lord intends us either to wait for a better time, or for more grace, or for a better gift. He wants us to have a true understanding that he is Being itself. And in this knowledge he wants our understanding to be grounded, with all our might and all our purpose and all our intention. It is on this ground that he wants us to take our place and make our home. . . .

Prayer is a right understanding of that fulness of joy that is to come, coupled with true longing and great trust. The tasting of the bliss for which we have been destined naturally makes us long for it. True understanding and love, together with sweet remembrance of the Savior, graciously makes us trust. So nature urges us to long, and grace to trust. And in these two activities our Lord keeps us constantly engaged because this is our duty. His goodness can assign nothing less to us than to make us diligently live up to what is our duty (indeed, it will seem to us nothing at all). This is exactly so; but if we do what we can and humbly ask for mercy and grace, then all that is lacking we shall find in him. And this is what he means when he says: "I am the ground of your praying."

(*Revelations* 42)

Our soul is God's dwelling place

Because of the great eternal love that God has for all humankind, he makes no distinction between the blessed soul of Christ
and the least soul that shall be saved. It is very easy to believe and to
trust that the indwelling of the blessed soul of Christ is very high in
the glorious Godhead. But it is also true, as I have understood from
what our Lord has shown me, that where the blessed soul of Christ
is, there is the substance of all souls that shall be saved by Christ.

How greatly we should rejoice that God indwells the soul. Yet
how much more should we rejoice that our soul dwells in God. Our
soul has been created to be God's dwelling place; and the dwelling
place of the soul is God, who is uncreated. It is a great illumination
inwardly to see and know that God our Creator dwells in our soul.
But it is a still much greater illumination inwardly to see and to
know that our soul, which is created, dwells in God's very
substance, and of this divine substance we are what we are.

(*Revelations* 54)

Knowing God and knowing ourselves

I saw with absolute certainty that it is easier and quicker for us
to know God than it is to know our own soul. For our soul is so
deeply grounded in God and so endlessly treasured that we
cannot come to know it until we first know God its Creator, to
whom it is united. Nevertheless, I saw that in order to reach
natural maturity we must have a wise and sincere desire to know
our soul, whereby we are taught to seek it where it is to be found,
that is, in God. So by the leading of the Holy Spirit through grace
we shall know both in one. It does not matter whether we are
moved to know God or our soul; both desires are good and true.

God is closer to us than our own soul. . . . So if we want to get to
know our soul and enter into communion and conversation with
it, we must seek it in our Lord God in whom it is enfolded.

(*Revelations* 56)

The city within

Then our good Lord opened my eyes and showed me my soul in the middle of my heart. I saw the soul as large as if it were an endless citadel and a blessed kingdom. From the condition that I saw it in I could tell that it is a glorious city. In the midst of that city sits our Lord Jesus, true God and true man, a handsome person and of tall stature, highest bishop, most majestic king and most glorious lord. I saw him arrayed with great pomp and honor. He sits in the soul always the same, in peace and in rest, and he rules and governs heaven and earth and all that exists. The manhood and the divinity sit in peace. The divinity rules and governs without any instrument or effort, and the soul is totally immersed in the blessed Godhead who is supreme power, supreme wisdom and supreme goodness.

The place that Jesus takes in our soul he will never leave again, as I see it, for in us is his homeliest home and his eternal dwelling. And in this vision he revealed the delight he had in creating the human soul. For as well as the Father had the power to make a creature, and as well as the Son had the knowledge to make a creature, so did the Holy Spirit want the human soul to be created. And so it was done. Therefore the Blessed Trinity rejoices without end in the creating of the human soul.

(Revelations 68)

The face of Christ who contemplates us, and we him

Glad and joyful and sweet is the blessed and lovely expression that our Lord shows to our soul, for he sees us always living in love-longing, and he wants our souls to turn cheerfully to him in order to give him his reward. And so I hope that, with his grace, he has and will ever more draw our outer expression to conform to our inner disposition, and make us all one with him and with each other, in that true eternal joy which is Jesus.

I see in our Lord's face three kinds of expression. The first is the expression of the Passion as he showed it when he was with us in this life at the time of his death. And although this sight is mournful and sorrowful, yet it remains glad and joyful because he is God. The second expression is pity, tenderness and compassion. This he shows to all lovers with the assurance of complete protection for those who are in need of his mercy. The third expression is that blessed face as it shall be without end. This was shown most often and continued for the longest period of time.

And so when we are in pain and distress he reveals to us the face of his Passion and cross, helping us to bear ours with his own blessed power. And when we sin he shows us the expression of pity and compassion, powerfully protecting us and defending us against all our enemies. These are the two usual expressions that he shows us in this life. Mixed with them is the third: namely, that blessed face partially like what it will be in heaven. This comes about by the touch of grace and the sweet enlightenment of the spiritual life, through which we are kept in true faith, hope and love, in contrition and devotion, as well as in contemplation and in all the different kinds of true joy and sweet consolations. The blessed face of God our Lord does all this in us through his grace. . . .

And ever the more clearly that the soul sees this blessed face by the grace of loving, the more it yearns to see it in fulness, that is, in its true likeness. For even though our Lord dwells now in us and is here with us, though he calls and enfolds us out of his tender love so that he can never leave us, though he is nearer to us than tongue can tell or heart can thirst; yet we shall never cease mourning and weeping, nor seeking nor longing, until we can clearly look at him in his blessed face. In that sight there can be no more grief nor any lack of well-being.

In this I saw cause for both laughter and tears. Cause for laughter because our Lord and Creator is so near to us and in us, and we in him through the fidelity with which he watches over us in his goodness.

Cause for tears because our spiritual eye is so blind, and we are so weighed down with the heaviness of our own mortal flesh and the darkness of sin, that we cannot clearly see the blessed face of our Lord and God. No, and because of this darkness, we can hardly believe or trust in his great love, nor be sure of his faithful protection of us. And it is for this reason that I say we can never cease mourning and weeping.

(*Revelations* 71, 72)

Our need and God's longing

I saw that God can provide everything we need. And the three things that I shall describe as needs are love, longing and pity. Pity born of love protects us in our time of need, and longing born from the same love draws us up to heaven. It is the thirst of God to love all humankind as a whole in himself, and in this thirst he has drawn the holy souls who are now in bliss. And he is always drawing and drinking and calling his living members, and yet he continues to thirst and long.

I saw three kinds of longing in God and they all have the same end. The first is God's longing to teach us to know him and love him ever more and more. The second is his longing to see us in bliss, as are the souls in heaven when they are freed from pain. The third is his longing to fill us with bliss, and that will be realized on the last day, when we shall be completely fulfilled for ever. I saw, as our faith teaches us, that on that day all pain and sorrow will be ended for those who shall be saved. And not only shall we receive the same bliss that the souls have received who are already in heaven, but we shall receive a new bliss which will flow richly out from God into us to fill us completely.

(*Revelations* 75)

The Question of Sin

God in a point

After this I saw God in a point (that is to say, in my mind), by which vision I saw that he is in all things. I looked at it carefully, seeing and recognizing through it that he does all that is done. I marvelled at this vision with a slight fear, and I thought "What is sin?" For I truly saw that God does all things, however small they may be. And I saw very clearly that nothing is done by chance or luck, but all is done by the foreseeing wisdom of God. If it seems like chance or luck in our eyes, the reason for that is our blindness and lack of foresight. For those things that are in God's foreseeing wisdom from all eternity, and which he so rightly and to his glory continually brings to their best conclusion, seem to fall on us out of the blue, catching us unawares. So in our blindness and lack of foresight we say: "It is all luck and chance." But to our Lord it is not so.

This is what I understood in this revelation of love; for I know well that in the eyes of our Lord God there is no chance or luck. This compelled me to admit that everything that is done is well done, for God our Lord does all.

At this time I was not shown the working of God's creatures, but only the working of God in his creatures. He is at the center of all, and he does everything. And I was certain that he does not sin. From this I understood that sin is not a deed, not a thing that is done, because in all this I was shown no sin. So I decided not to go on wondering and puzzling about this matter but to look at the Lord to see what he would show me. . . .

This vision was shown to teach me that our Lord wants the soul to turn around and sincerely contemplate him and all his works. For they are totally good, and all his decrees are easy and sweet.

(*Revelations* 11)

All shall be well

Our Lord brought to mind the longing I had for him earlier, and I saw that nothing hindered me except sin. This I saw to be true in general for all of us. And I thought to myself: "If there had been no sin we should all have been pure and clean like our Lord, as he created us." And so in my foolishness, before this time, I had often wondered why God, with his great foresight and wisdom, did not prevent the business of sin in the first place. For then, I thought, all would have been well.

This curious wondering would have been better left alone, but instead I mourned and sorrowed over it without reason and discretion. But Jesus, who in this vision instructed me in all that I needed to know, answered me with this word and said: "Sin is necessary; but all shall be well, and all manner of things shall be well."

By this bare word "sin" our Lord meant me to understand in general all that is not good. It included the shameful contempt and the uttermost tribulation that our Lord endured for us in this life, his death with all its pains, and the suffering of all his creatures both in spirit and in body. For all of us are at times distressed, and we shall continue to be so, like Jesus our master, until we are wholly purified in our mortal flesh, and in all our interior affections that are not wholly good.

And in this sight, with all the pains that ever were or ever shall be, I understood the Passion of Christ to be the greatest pain, far surpassing every other pain. All this was shown to me in an instant of time, and quickly passed over into comfort. For our good Lord did not want the soul to be frightened by this ugly sight. But "sin" itself I did not see, because I believe that it does not have its own substance or any form of being; nor can it be known except by the pain it causes.

It seems to me that this pain is something very real and it lasts for a while, because it purifies us, makes us know ourselves and ask for mercy. But the Passion of our Lord is a comfort to us in all this, and this is his blessed will. Because of the tender love that our Lord has for those who are to be saved, he gives comfort quickly and sweetly, his meaning being: "Yes, it is true that sin is the root and cause of all pain. But all shall be well, and all manner of things shall be well."

These words were revealed to me most tenderly, without any kind of blame either toward me or anybody else who shall be saved. It would therefore indeed be unbecoming of me to blame God or question him about my sin, since he does not blame me for it.

And in these same words I say a wonderful and most profound mystery hidden in God, which will be clearly made known to us in heaven. When we shall know this mystery, then we shall truly know why he allowed sin to come and, knowing that, we shall rejoice with him for ever.

(*Revelations* 27)

Christ's compassion for us and our's for one another

Yes, I saw clearly that our Lord even rejoices with pity and compassion over the tribulations of his servants. And on each person whom he loves and wants to bring to bliss, he lays something that in his eyes is not a defect yet makes them to be humiliated, despised, scorned, mocked and rejected in this world. And this he does to prevent them from being harmed by the pomp, the pride, and the vainglory of this wretched life, and to better prepare them for the way that will bring them to heaven with infinite joy and eternal bliss. For he says: "I shall completely break you of your empty affections and your vicious pride; and then I shall gather you together and make you humble and gentle, pure and holy, through oneing you to me."

And then I saw that every natural compassion that anyone has for a fellow-Christian is due to Christ living within them. . . .

He also wants us to see that he is our ground, and that his pains and tribulations so far exceed all that we can suffer that they cannot be fully understood.

Taking good notice of this will prevent us from grumbling and despairing in our own suffering. It makes us see truly that our sin deserves it, but his love excuses us. And in his great courtesy he does away with our blame and looks upon us with pity and compassion, as innocent and beloved children.

(*Revelations* 28)

"I will keep you safe"

God reminded me that I would fall into sin, but because of the delight that I felt in the contemplation of him I did not immediately pay attention to this revelation. However, our Lord most mercifully waited and gave me the grace to pay attention. At first I applied this revelation just to myself; but by the gracious comfort that followed, as you will see, I was taught to apply it to all my fellow-Christians.

Even though our Lord showed me that I would sin, by "me alone" is meant all. And in this I felt a gentle fear rising in me, to which our Lord answered: "I keep you very safe." This word was spoken to me with love and a guarantee of spiritual protection greater than I can or may tell. For just as I was first shown that I would sin, so I was shown comfort, protection and security for all my fellow Christians. What could make me love my fellow Christians more than to see in God that he loves all who are going to be saved as if they were one soul?

For in every soul that shall be saved there is a godly will which has never said yes to sin, nor ever will. Just as there is an animal will in the lower part of us which can will no good, so there is a godly will in the higher part of us which is so good it can never will any evil, but only good. Therefore, we are those whom he loves, and we endlessly do what pleases him.

And this our good Lord showed in the fullness of love in which we stand before him. Yes, he himself loves us now, while we are here on earth, just as much as he will love us when we are before his blessed face. It is only because we are lacking in love that we have so many difficulties.

And God showed me that sin shall not be to our shame but to our honor, because just as there rightly is a corresponding pain for every sin, so likewise there is given to the same soul by love a blessing for every sin. Just as different sins are punished with different pains according to their seriousness, likewise they shall be rewarded with different joys in heaven.

(*Revelations* 37, 38)

God protects us even when we sin

Our good Lord protects us most tenderly when it seems to us that we are almost forsaken and cast off because of our sins, and because we see that we have deserved it. Yet because of the humility that we learn from this we are raised very high in God's sight by his grace. Furthermore, those whom our Lord chooses he invites through his special grace with such great contrition, compassion and true longing for the will of God, that they are suddenly delivered from sin and pain, taken up to bliss, and made equal to the saints.

By contrition we are made clean, by compassion we are made ready, and by true longing for God we are made worthy. These are the three means, as I see it, by which all souls get to heaven; that is to say, those who on earth have been sinners and are destined to be saved.

For every sinful soul must be healed by these medicines. And even though the sinner is healed, the wounds the sinner bears are seen by God not as wounds but as signs of honor. And so we see things upside down. As we are punished here on earth with sorrow and penance, so we shall be rewarded in heaven by the courteous love of our Almighty God, who wishes that none of those who come there lose in any way the benefits gained from their struggles. For he regards sin as sorrow and pain for those who love him; and to them, out of love, he attributes no blame. . . .

It is a sign of the supreme friendship of our courteous Lord that he should keep hold of us so tenderly while we are in our sin. Furthermore, he touches us most secretly and shows us our sin in the sweet light of his mercy and grace. But when we see ourselves so foul, then we think that God should be angry with us on account of our sin. Then by means of contrition we are inspired by the Holy Spirit to pray and to desire with all our might to amend our life in order to still God's anger, until we are able to find rest of soul and peace of conscience. Then we hope that God has forgiven us our sin—and he really has.

Our courteous Lord then shows himself to the soul with a joyful and happy expression and in a friendly, welcoming way, as if the soul had come out of imprisonment and suffering, saying: "My darling, I am glad that you have come to me. I have always been with you in all your troubles, and now you see me loving you, and we are made one in bliss."

This is how sins are forgiven by grace and mercy, and our soul honorably and joyfully received—just as it will be when it comes to heaven. This happens whenever the soul experiences the gracious working of the Holy Spirit and the power of Christ's passion.

(*Revelations* 39, 40)

There is no anger in God

I saw very clearly that where our Lord appears there comes peace and there is no place for anger. I could not see any kind of anger in God, neither short-lived nor long-lasting. For truly, as I see it, if God were angry even for a moment we could have neither life, nor place, nor being. As truly as we have our being from the eternal power of God and from the eternal wisdom and the eternal goodness, just as truly we have our safe-keeping in the eternal power of God, in the eternal wisdom and in the eternal goodness. Though we may feel anger and disagreement and strife within ourselves, yet we are all enfolded in God's mildness and humility, God's kindness and graciousness.

I saw very clearly that all our salvation, our friendship, our home, our life and our being are in God. The same everlasting goodness that keeps hold of us when we sin, so that we do not perish, is the same everlasting goodness that continually gives us peace, instead of all our anger and perverse feelings.

It also makes us see with true fear our desperate need to seek God's forgiveness and in his grace to long for salvation. We cannot be blessedly saved until we are truly in peace and in love, for that is our salvation.

Although our blindness and weakness have allowed the anger and rebellion that is in us to lead us into hardship, distress and suffering, yet we are kept perfectly safe by God's merciful love so that we do not perish. . . .

So I saw that God is our true peace and our sure protector when we ourselves are not at peace; and he constantly works to bring us to everlasting peace.

(*Revelations* 49)

The Motherhood of God

The Holy Trinity—Father, Mother, Lord

I saw and understood that the high power of the Trinity is our Father, and the deep wisdom of the Trinity is our Mother, and the great love of the Trinity is our Lord.

Our Father wills, our Mother works, our Lord the Holy Spirit confirms. Therefore we must love our God in whom we have our being. We must reverently thank and praise him for creating us, fervently praying to our Mother for mercy and compassion, and to our Lord the Holy Spirit for help and grace. For in these three is our life: nature, mercy and grace. From these we have gentleness, patience, pity, and hatred of sin and wickedness, for it is in the nature of virtue to hate sin and wickedness.

So Jesus is our true mother in nature through creating us in the first place; and he is our true mother in grace through taking on our created nature. All the loving service and all the sweet and gentle offices of the precious motherhood are proper to the Second Person; for in him we have this "godly will" whole and safe for ever, both in nature and in grace, by his own innate goodness.

I saw that the motherhood of God can be contemplated in three ways. The first is to consider the ground of our nature's creation. The second is the assumption of our nature, from which stems the motherhood of grace. The third is the motherhood at work. And from this, sustained by the same mercy, it spreads forth in endless length and breadth, height and depth. And all is one love.

(*Revelations* 59)

Jesus our true mother

Our mother in nature (who is also our mother in grace because he truly wanted to become our mother in all things) began his work in complete humility and gentleness in the Virgin's womb. He revealed this in the first Revelation when he brought that gentle Virgin before my mind's eye in the simple condition in which she found herself when she conceived.

That is to say, in this humble place our great God, the supreme wisdom of all things, arrayed himself in our poor flesh and fully prepared himself to do the work and service of motherhood in all things. The service of the mother is nearest, readiest and most reliable. Its nearness is because it is most natural; its readiness is because it is most loving; and its reliability is because it is most true. No one might or ever could perform this office perfectly except him alone. We know that our mothers bear us for pain and death. But what is it that Jesus our true mother does? He who is all-love bears us for joy and eternal life. Blessed may he be! So he sustained us and carried us within him in love and in labor until the fullness of time, when he wanted to suffer the sharpest thorns and the most cruel pains that have ever been and ever shall be, until at the end he died. And when he had finished and had given birth to us for bliss, even then his most wonderful love was not satisfied, as he revealed in these high and surpassing words of love: "If I could suffer more I would suffer more."

He could not die any more but he would not cease working. So he had to feed us, for the most precious love of motherhood has placed this obligation toward us upon him. The human mother suckles her child with her own milk, but our precious mother Jesus can feed us with himself, and he does this most constantly and tenderly by means of the Blessed Sacrament, which is the precious food of true life. . . .

The human mother can put her child tenderly to her breast, but our tender mother Jesus can lead us intimately into his blessed breast through the sweet open wound in his side, and there gives us a glimpse of the Godhead and the joy of heaven, with the inner certainty of bliss. . . .

This fair and lovely word "mother" is so sweet and gentle in itself that it cannot truly be said of anyone or to anyone except of him and to him, who is the true mother of life and of all things. The properties of motherhood are: natural love, wisdom and knowledge. And this is God. Though it is true that our physical giving birth is but little, humble and simple compared to our spiritual birth, yet it is still he who is at work when his creatures give birth.

A kind, loving mother, who knows and understands the needs of her child, guards it most tenderly as the nature and state of motherhood demand. And always as the child grows in stature she changes her methods but not her love. When it gets older she allows it to be chastised in order to break down its faults and to enable the child to accept values and graces. This, along with everything that is lovely and good, is our Lord's work in those who do it.

So he is our mother in nature by means of the working of grace in the lower part, out of love for the higher part. And he wants us to know this, for he wants us to fasten all our love onto him. In all this, I saw that every duty that we have toward fatherhood or motherhood by the command of God, is fulfilled in truly loving God; and this blessed love Christ produces in us. . . .

The mother may sometimes allow her child to fall and be hurt in different ways for its own benefit; but because of her love she could never allow her child to suffer any serious harm. And even if our earthly mother may allow her child to die, our heavenly mother, Jesus, can never allow us, his children, to die; for he is all mighty, all wise and all love. There is no one like him. Blessed may he be!

(*Revelations* 60-61)

The Meaning of All
the Revelations–Julian's Conclusion

Love was his meaning

From the time I first had these revelations I often longed to know what our Lord meant. More than fifteen years later I was given in response a spiritual understanding and was told: "Do you want to know what our Lord meant in all this? Know it well: Love was his meaning. Who showed it to you? Love. What did he show you? Love. Why did he show it to you? For love. Remain firm in this love and you will taste it ever more deeply, but you will never know anything else from it forever and ever.

So I was taught that Love is what our Lord meant. And I saw with absolute certainty in this revelation and in all the rest, that before God made us he loved us, and that his love has never slackened and never will. In this love he has done all his works. In this love he has made all things for our benefit, and in this love our life is everlasting. In our creation we had a beginning, but the love in which he created us was in him forever without beginning. In this love we have our beginning. And all this we shall see in God without end.

Thanks be to God. Here ends the book of *Revelations* of Julian the anchoress of Norwich, on whose soul may God have mercy.

(*Revelations* 86)

Bibliography & For Further Reading

Texts

Angela of Foligno. *Complete Works*. Translated and with an Introduction by Paul Lachance. New York: Paulist Press, 1993.

Birgitta of Sweden, *Life and Selected Revelations*. Translated by Albert Ryle Kezel. New York: Paulist Press, 1990.

Gertrude of Helfta, *The Herald of Divine Love*. Translated and edited by Margaret Winkworth. New York: Paulist Press, 1993.

Julian of Norwich, *Showings*. Translated and with an Introduction by E. Colledge & J. Walsh. New York: Paulist Press, 1978.

Julian of Norwich. *Showing of Love*. Translated from the BL Sloane 2499 Ms, collated with the Westminster Cathedral Ms, the Paris, Bibliotheque Nationale, Anglais Ms & the BL, Additional 37, 790, Amherst Ms by Julia Bolton Holloway. London: DLT 2003.

Background Reading and Anthologies

Armstrong, K. *The English Mystics of the Fourteenth Century*. London: Kyle Cathie, 1991.

Clay, R.M. *The Hermits and Anchorites of England*. London: Methuen, 1914.

De Sola Chervin, R. *Prayers of the Women Mystics*. Ann Arbor, MI: Servant Publications, 1992.

Furlong, M. *Visions and Longings, Medieval Women Mystics*. London: Mowbray, 1996.

Gosset, T. *Women Mystics of the Medieval Era: An Anthology*. Translated by Wendy Brennan. London: St. Pauls, 2003.

Jones, E.A. ed. *The Medieval Mystical Tradition in England: Papers Read at Charney Manor, July 2004* (Exeter Symposium VII). Cambridge: D.S. Brewer, 2004.

Lachance, P. *Angela of Foligno, Passionate Mystic of the Double Abyss*. New City Press, 2006.

McGinn, B. *The Flowering of Mysticism, Men and Women in the New Mysticism—1200-1350*. New York: Crossroad Herder, 1998.

Murk-Jansen, S. *Brides in the Desert, The Spirituality of the Beguines*. London: Darton, Longman & Todd, 1998.

Oden, A. ed. *In Her Words, Women's Writings in the History of Christian Thought*. London: SPCK, 1995.

Raitt, J. ed. *Christian Spirituality in the High Middle Ages and Reformation*. London: SCM, 1988.

Renevey, D. and Whitehead C. eds. *Writing Religious Women: Female & Textual Practices in Late Medieval England*. Cardiff: University of Wales Press, 2000.

Savage, A. and Watson, N., trans. *Anchoritic Spirituality, Ancrene Wisse and Associated Works*. New York: Paulist Press, 1991.

Schmitt, M. & Kulzer L. ed. *Medieval Women Monastics*. Collegeville: Liturgical Press, 1996.

Waal E.de, A. *Life-Giving Way, A Commentary of the Rule of Saint Benedict*. London: Chapman, 1995.

Acknowledgments

I would like to thank Paulist Press for permission to quote from their translations of the works of Saint Gertrude, Blessed Angela of Foligno and Saint Birgitta of Sweden in the Classics of Western Spirituality series. Also Josef Pichler for the use of his own translation of Julian's *Revelations of Divine Love*.

ALSO AVAILABLE IN THE SAME SERIES FROM NEW CITY PRESS

AELRED OF RIEVAULX—THE WAY OF FRIENDSHIP
M. BASIL PENNINGTON (ed.)
ISBN 1-56548-128-3-0, 2d printing, paper, 168 pp.

**ANGELA OF FOLIGNO—PASSIONATE MYSTIC
OF THE DOUBLE ABYSS**
PAUL LACHANCE (ed.)
ISBN 978-1-56548-248-7, paper, 128 pp.

BERNARD OF CLAIRVAUX—A LOVER TEACHING THE WAY OF LOVE
M. BASIL PENNINGTON (ed.)
ISBN 1-56548-089-9, 3d printing, paper, 128 pp.

CATHERINE OF SIENA—PASSION FOR THE TRUTH ...
MARY O'DRISCOLL, O.P. (ed.)
ISBN 1-56548-235-2, 7th printing, paper, 144 pp.

FRANCIS DE SALES—FINDING GOD WHEREVER YOU ARE
JOSEPH F. POWER, O.S.F.S. (ed.)
ISBN 1-56548-074-0, 5th printing, paper, 160 pp.

JOHN HENRY NEWMAN—HEART SPEAKS TO HEART
LAWRENCE S. CUNNINGHAM (ed.)
ISBN 1-56548-193-3, paper, 128 pp.

JOHN OF THE CROSS—THE ASCENT TO JOY
MARC FOLEY, O.C.D. (ed.)
ISBN 1-56548-174-7, 2d printing, paper, 152 pp.

JULIAN OF NORWICH—JOURNEYS INTO JOY
JOHN NELSON (ed.)
ISBN 1-56548-134-8, 2d printing, paper, 184 pp.

MARTIN LUTHER—FAITH IN CHRIST AND THE GOSPEL
ERIC W. GRITSCH (ed.)
ISBN 1-56548-041-4, 2d printing, paper, 192 pp.